AUTHOR'S NOTE

If you want a reassuring voice
the whole book to you, so we

Once you've bought the book, y
back, to access the full free audi
keep the content secure.

When you buy *The Big Secret of How*, you're also helping to support educational charities I'm involved with in India and South Africa. Thank you!

The audiobook is completely optional to use. Go it alone, or we can read it together. You decide.

🎧 As a taster, you can listen to the Prologue read by me here, no sign-up needed. Just scan the QR code.

CONTENTS

Prologue   9

Introduction   15

PART ONE
POSITIVE MENTAL FITNESS AND HAPPINESS
Rewire Your Brain for Success   25

SECRET #1 How to Find Happiness   31
SECRET #2 How to Change Your Life   34
SECRET #3 How to Find Peace   37

CONTEMPLATION CORNER   40

SECRET #4 How to Keep Your Mind Balanced   42
SECRET #5 How to Look Great   45
SECRET #6 How to Be Free from Fear   47
SECRET #7 How to Conquer the Mind   51

CONTEMPLATION CORNER   53

REFLECTIONS   55

MOTIVATION ZONE   57

PART TWO
MEDITATION, MINDFULNESS & YOGA
Calm the Chaos Within   65

Secret #8 How to Calm the Mind   73
Secret #9 How to Meditate   75
Secret #10 How to Balance Your Energy   80
Secret #11 How to Breathe   84
Secret #12 How to Practise Yoga to Reset The Mind   87

CONTEMPLATION CORNER   90

Secret #13 How to Be Mindful in Daily Life   94
Secret #14 How to Survive a Day in Silence   97
Secret #15 How to Stay Positive   100

CONTEMPLATION CORNER   103

REFLECTIONS   106

MOTIVATION ZONE   109

PART THREE
LOVE SELF-LOVE & FAMILY
Build Relationships that Matter   115

Secret #16 How to Attract Your Ideal Partner   122
Secret #17 How to Bring More Love into Your Life   125

CONTEMPLATION CORNER   129

Secret #18 How to Stay Connected with Your Family   131
Secret #19 How to Increase Your Faith   136
Secret #20 How to Love Yourself Unconditionally   139

CONTEMPLATION CORNER   142

REFLECTIONS   144

MOTIVATION ZONE   147

PART FOUR
PURPOSE WISDOM & FREEDOM
Discover your Unique Path   151

Secret #21 How to Discover Your Purpose   156
Secret #22 How to Be Wise   158
Secret #23 How to Be Free   161

CONTEMPLATION CORNER   166

Secret #24 How to Stay True to Yourself   168
Secret #25 How to Stay Calm in an Argument   172
Secret #26 How to Be a Great Leader   175

CONTEMPLATION CORNER   178

THE BIG SECRET OF HOW

to find happy meaningful success

DAVID GREEN

Publisher: Masters & Son Limited, Guernsey, Channel Islands

This publication includes optional access to free companion audio material, created and recorded by the author. The audio content is protected by the same copyright and intellectual property laws as the text of this book. Access is provided for no extra charge via QR code after purchase of either the e-book or the paperback. A brief sign-up is required to help prevent unauthorised distribution. Paid versions of audio may also be available through main audio book carriers.

Audio Production: Offbeat Audio

Typesetting: Ramesh Kumar Pitchai

ISBN 978-0-9926487-3-2

REFLECTIONS   181

MOTIVATION ZONE   188

PART FIVE
SUCCESS AMBITION & CAREER
Create a Career that Counts   195

Secret #27 How to Be a Great Success   201
Secret #28 How to Find Meaningful Success   204
Secret #29 How to Become an Entrepreneur   207
Secret #30 How to Make a Profit   209
Secret #31 How to Sell Your Business   213

CONTEMPLATION CORNER   215

Secret #32 How to Negotiate your Salary   218
Secret #33 How to Think Like a Spiritual Billionaire 221
Secret #34 How to Master the Art of Humility   223

CONTEMPLATION CORNER   226

REFLECTIONS   228

MOTIVATION ZONE   232

PART SIX
SELF-AWARENESS PERSONAL GROWTH & HEALTH
Optimise your Wellbeing   237

Secret #35 How to Live a Conscious Life   242
Secret #36 How to Deal with Bullies   246
Secret #37 How to Avoid Negative Thoughts   249
Secret #38 How to Spend Money Consciously   252
Secret #39 How to Live in Truth   255

CONTEMPLATION CORNER   258

Secret #40 How to Be a Healthy Vegan   261
Secret #41 How to Make the Best Hummus   264
Secret #42 How to Stop Eating Animals   266

CONTEMPLATION CORNER   268

REFLECTIONS   271

MOTIVATION ZONE   275

PART SEVEN
INSPIRATION MANIFESTATION & MOTIVATION
Turn Insights into Action   281

Secret #43 How to Be Inspired   291
Secret #44 How to Unleash Your Unlimited Potential   293
Secret #45 How to Create a Routine That Brings Success   296

CONTEMPLATION CORNER   299

Secret #46 How to Manifest Your Destiny   301
Secret #47 How to Land Your Dream Job   304
Secret #48 How to Laugh at Failure   308
Secret #49 How to Lead a Life of Tranquillity   311
Secret #50 How to Make Your Dreams a Reality   314

CONTEMPLATION CORNER   317

REFLECTIONS   319

MOTIVATION ZONE   322

INSPIRATION CORNER   327

FINAL REFLECTIONS   328

ENJOY THE FREE AUDIO!   329

AFTERWORD   330

DEDICATION   332

ABOUT THE FRONT COVER   332

THE LOTUS FLOWER   332

ABOUT THE AUTHOR   333

ACKNOWLEDGEMENTS   334

PROLOGUE

Pour yourself a cuppa.

Kick off your shoes.

Put your feet up.

Relax.

Take a minute or two - just for you.

Gently breathe - in and out of the nose.

Anchor yourself in the flow of the moment.

Feel the life-force in each breath...

The key to instant calmness.

Now that we've shared a quiet moment together, let's get straight to the heart of the matter -what we're really all after - *happy, meaningful success*.

What exactly is *happy, meaningful success*?

Is it really possible to attain without taking life too seriously?

Happy, meaningful success brings love, joy and well-being for us and others - an extraordinary mix of gratitude, kindness and integrity.

Happy, meaningful success spreads love and goodness, extending a helping hand to everyone.

If we want to live fulfilled, contented lives, that make a positive impact on the planet, we must...

☆ Challenge ourselves to take an honest look at our behaviour and habits.

☆ Make the mind our servant and not our master.

☆ Contemplate deeply what we do and why we do it.

☆ Be kind to ourselves as we change and grow.

True reflection is the rocket fuel to success. It infuses us with purpose, power and positive intentions - to manifest dynamic action, not just on New Year's Day, but each and every day.

To catalyse change, we need confidence and courage.

We need to know HOW.

We need PURPOSE, FOCUS, TRANSFORMATION and ENTHUSIASM to achieve lasting success.

When we understand HOW, we can then ask WHY.

Finding Your Truth Starts Here

Keep yourself in the flow of the moment. Calmly read out loud and ask yourself:

☆ What's the point of dreaming if my dreams do not become my reality?

☆ What's the point of working, day in day out, when freedom feels so far away?

☆ What's the point of measuring my career success, but never measuring my happiness?

☆ What's the point of enduring constant stress and unhappiness just to exist?

☆ What's the point of following a path that does not make me feel truly, deeply happy?

Pause for a moment. Let the questions and your honest answers sink in. *Listen* to your feelings.

If you're struggling to find your voice, if you're filled with doubt or a bit dejected, you're not alone. Most of us have been there.

If you feel stuck in the same old *Broken Dreams* movie, caught in a loop of old disappointments, set your doubts aside for now.

This moment will pass. Be kind to yourself.

My Realisation

I wish someone had encouraged me to ask these questions earlier in my life. To learn how to check in with my feelings. When I reflect, I was conditioned from an early age to suppress any feelings. Life was all about working hard, achievements and ticking boxes - *success, marriage, more success.* Honestly, I wasn't really *living.* Productive and driven, but deep down, like a robot - programmed and focussed on ambition and financial success but emotionally shut down - numb to my feelings.

And when I contemplate deeply, I realise that I'm normally asked, "What do you think?" or "What would you do in my position?"

Very few people ever ask me, "How do *you* feel?"

Even if I'd been asked this at the height of my career, I would have dismissed the question out of hand. I was never taught how to stop, to just feel. Only to proceed and succeed.

If no one has ever asked you lately - or ever - let me be the first...

How are *you* feeling, right now?

Take your time to reflect. Pause for a moment. Relax. Listen to the secret wisdom inside. It will come.

Sunrise on Day Zero

To discover our true feelings, we have to take a leap of faith - to visit *Day Zero.*

That's the moment of reckoning we can't avoid. The impact moment too often forced upon us by illness, burnout, heartbreak or disappointment. Then and only then, do we realise there's nowhere to hide. We have no choice. We are forced to stop. To stop talking about our problems - instead, to start solving them.

My most profound *Day Zero?*

Spending 300 days in silence. The challenge that changed everything.

No internet. No news. No talking.
No daily schedule. No distractions.
No TV. No friends. No family.

During that silence challenge, I found powerful tools to conquer life's chaos - tools I will share with you in the book.

You'll learn how to...

☆ Break the cycle of negative thoughts
☆ How to calm your mind and body and
☆ Uncover what's driving you
☆ How to realise your dreams - at warp speed and
☆ Reset your mind with positivity - using meditation, mindfulness and powerful affirmations
☆ How to tap into the power of silence

And don't worry. You won't need to go into 300 days of silence. I promise.

The Zen Button

I've asked you some challenging questions. So, now's a good time to press *The Zen Button.*

It's a tool I use to shift the mental clutter, negative thoughts and unhelpful emotions. Think of it as your inner emergency brake. When problems overwhelm you or stress creeps in, pause and press. You can use *The Zen Button* to calm yourself and infuse power and calmness. It's the perfect way to reset your mind. *And,* when combined with affirmations, a powerful mental and emotional shift is triggered.

By using affirmations, we speak directly to every part of our being. Imprinting our vision - transforming doubts and fears into optimism and self-belief.

If affirmations are new to you, think of them as mental sit-ups in the gymnasium of the mind. Science shows that voicing our goals fires up the prefrontal cortex, the 'get-it-done' action- planner of the brain.

When you press *The Zen Button*, always anchor yourself in the flow of the moment.
Sit straight. Let your energy flow naturally from the top to the bottom of the spine.
Witness each breath - gently being pulled by the life-force in and out of the nose.
Let the breath find its rhythm. No need to control. Time to let go.
Gently pay attention - just above the eyebrows - a little inside.
Be still. Be the witness. Sit calmly.
Now say aloud these affirmations - with purpose, intention and a smile...

☆ I promise myself to make my dreams a reality, with every breath.
☆ I promise myself to create meaning and fulfilment, in my work, daily.
☆ I promise myself to pursue lasting happiness and true freedom, with courage, in every moment.

☆ I promise myself to speak my truth and to express my feelings openly, starting now.

☆ I promise myself to be kind and compassionate to me and others, in all that I do.

Feel the shift? Repeat until you do. Practise daily. Set a time in the morning or the evening. Stick to it.

The Big Secret to Empower Affirmations

To become mindful of the life-force in every breath, direct your awareness to the space just inside the forehead above the eyebrows. Conscious connection to the pituitary gland, the master gland - the gateway to enlightenment in Buddhist and yogic traditions.

We're only at the start of the book.

If you're ready...

To ask the big questions and find the big answers...

To create your own *Self-Help Master Plan* to achieve *happy, meaningful success*, lasting transformation and deep contentment...

To connect with your inner voice of wisdom...

To face your truth and fearlessly pursue your dreams...

To be challenged, inspired and motivated...

To live life to the fullest, smiling every step of the way...

Then this book is for you.

Grab a pen. It's interactive.

Open your mind. You're about to unlock your own secret wisdom.

Invest in yourself. Start meeting tomorrow's destiny - *Today.*

Turn the page. You're about to meet the version of yourself that's already free.

This book might just be the ONE that transports you to your *aha* moment - the moment everything changes.

INTRODUCTION

A Quick Word Before We Begin

Before we dive in further, a few words about beliefs. You'll find ideas in this book drawn from various traditions and my personal experiences - yogic, spiritual, ancient and modern wisdom. Some are practical tools; others may sound unfamiliar at first. You don't have to believe in God, chakras or enlightenment to benefit. I certainly didn't when I started to meditate.

Whatever your beliefs - whether you find comfort in science, religion, spirituality or simple common sense - everything here is shared with one aim: to quieten down the noise inside, reconnect with what matters to you and make space for change. Take what resonates and leave the rest behind, but staying open might just be the inspiration you need right now.

That's the essence of the book. To listen to yourself, try out a few new ideas and see what shifts.

Who Am I?

I think about life a lot. Why are we here? What makes us tick? Why do we think, speak and act as we do? How can we *really* manifest our maximum potential and fulfil our desires?

What's our *true purpose*?

The Silence Challenge

As you now know, a few years ago, I embarked upon an unusual challenge. One that only a handful of people in the world have even considered. To go into silence indefinitely. To search for the hidden answers to life's burning questions.

You're probably also searching...

...for ways to transform the *imaginary* YOU into the REAL YOU...

...to achieve and realise your dreams - perhaps to find your perfect partner - to be successful, happy and content. To live a meaningful life.

Some people jump out of aeroplanes, climb mountains or run back-to-back marathons to push themselves beyond their limits. My challenge was to go into silence, locked away from daily life. Shut off from society. Far from home. Alone. No time limit.

The goal was clear. To test myself. To know myself. To find out what would happen in silence.

Would I be calm and balanced or overwhelmed with sadness and loneliness?

I lasted 300 days.

I had survived the *Wolf of Wall Street* world of bond trading and the relentless pressure as a young entrepreneur, building a business from scratch to sale, which hit £100 million turnover.

But nothing in my armoury could prepare me to be cut off from society.

Day after day, week after week, month after month.

Nothing could soothe the loneliness.

By the end, I wondered if I'd be able to speak again. Words began to feel forgotten, like they no longer existed.

Silence strips everything away. No distractions. No escape from the mind, the boredom, the inevitable unhappiness. Just me and the present moment. In the darkest moments, I could see myself. Who I really am - a messy mix of love, pain, suffering and ego. That's when the profound revelations came...

How to cultivate inner happiness when my mind was unhappy.

How boredom can turn into wisdom.

How to ride the waves of disruptive thoughts without being controlled by them.

How to boost my positive energy...

...to find calmness through meditation.

...to overcome mental pain and suffering by becoming the silent witness.

...to love myself as I am.

HOW to simply JUST BE.

In silence, everything becomes clearer. Good and bad thoughts dissolve into the silence.

I witnessed how easily we give away our power, by reacting defensively or with anger, when triggered by others. I kept a daily diary during silence. Some entries were longer than others, but every day, I jotted down a *thought of the day*. You'll find some of these reflections from the 300 days of silence woven into the book, alongside tools and gentle nudges to encourage you to rediscover your own unique path.

Hang on. Hit the pause button for a second. Time-out. Forget the polished intro. If you think I've got it all worked out, think again. Doubted by others who put you down behind your back? Worried about your job or feeling inadequate? Join the club. I failed Economics and Physics. No degree. I was made redundant. It made me more determined. If that sounds familiar, you're in the right place.

Stress is a lingering shadow that follows us around. As a bond trader, every time I made a price in the bedlam of the trading floor, I prayed I had made the correct price. I saw grown men break down in tears after being publicly shamed for a single error. Executive directors would host a drinks party on a Friday, only to find their desks cleared before they went home; a new face installed by 7am on Monday, ready to lead the morning traders' meeting. No questions asked. No explanations given.

To fellow entrepreneurs and go-getters - don't lose heart. When I started my business at 23, the 'experts' told me I would fail. Trust yourself and choose your advisors carefully. Ambition has a cost. If you're going to pay the price of success, make sure you invest equally in your wellbeing. Meditation is the best investment I ever made.

Emotionally, we all face challenges, whether it be divorce, break-ups, being part of a dysfunctional family, loneliness, illness or financial difficulties.

If you're in that place, you're not alone.

When our world is crashing around us, so often we feel ill-equipped, sometimes paralysed - at a loss to know what to do. In these moments, family dynamics can come into play. Parents may ask what they did wrong, without taking a look at themselves. Children may wonder why their parents are so stressed and unhappy.

The truth is, we're influenced by the choices of our parents - some made wisely, some reckless and others without much thought of the consequences. As adults, many of us are left carrying the fallout, while our parents who shaped us, may not see the need to reflect, or simply lack the emotional awareness or resilience to do so. That leaves us with two choices. To follow the pattern of our parents, or to find the tools, the strength, and the love around us to break any deep-seated negative patterns from childhood.

If you come from a loving, emotionally strong family, cherish it. You're lucky. Never take it for granted.

Mindset Mastery: How Meditation Changes Everything

I've practised meditation daily for 30 years. I never missed a day. You might find that hard to picture, but think about it: do you ever forget to eat, shower or brush your teeth every day? Meditation nourishes, restores and resets the mind.

Believe me, I was the last person in the world to sit still and meditate.

Impatient. Restless. Agitated. Stressed out.

Dogmatic. Definitely not *Godmatic*.

My first meditation class? Incense burning. Sitting in a circle of people. Everyone chanting OM. Me thinking, ERR-UM. The teacher saying, *Just breathe*. Me thinking, *What else have we been doing all of our lives*?! I nearly ran out of the room.

Another time, I started laughing in front of a guru during meditation. He smiled and said, "Laughter is good, laughter is God!" Now that's my kind of wisdom. Laughter, love and encouragement!

On a more serious note, I can 100% guarantee that if meditation works for me, it will work for you. It's the best rescue remedy I found to escape the chaos and noise inside my head.

Now where were we?

Inside *The Big Secret of How*, you'll discover fifty *secrets* - a mix of insights and truths. A few crumbs of wisdom and a touch of humour. Growth should feel inspiring and joyful, not depressing and heavy.

Finding clarity and wisdom doesn't have to be another boring chore. We've enough of those already. At least I do...

Searching for my phone and glasses at the same time - when I need my glasses to find my phone!

Discovering my favourite new t-shirt has *shrunk* - because the vegan brownies on holiday insisted I eat them.

What bugs *you* the most?

Now's Your Moment

This is your chance to take a much-needed time-out. To reflect honestly and take inspired action. To finally alchemise your dreams into the meaningful success you crave and deserve. To tap into the power already inside, without taking life too seriously.

To break free from imagination and live in realisation.

How to Use This Book

The Big Secret of How is your easy-to-follow *roadmap to contentment*, divided into seven parts:

1) POSITIVE MENTAL FITNESS & HAPPINESS — *Rewire Your Brain for Success*

2) MEDITATION, MINDFULNESS & YOGA — *Calm the Chaos Within*

3) LOVE, SELF-LOVE & FAMILY — *Build Relationships That Matter*

4) PURPOSE, WISDOM & FREEDOM — *Discover Your Unique Path*

5) SUCCESS, AMBITION & CAREER — *Create a Career That Counts*

6) SELF-AWARENESS, PERSONAL GROWTH & HEALTH — *Optimise Your Wellbeing*

7) INSPIRATION, MANIFESTATION & MOTIVATION — *Turn Insights into Action*

A Moment to Pause

At first glance, some topics may grab you more than others. But as Aristotle points out, "the whole is greater than the sum of the parts."

The key to meaningful personal development is to embrace all areas of your life, even those you'd rather avoid. Lasting change comes from honest self-reflection, balanced with self-compassion, self-love and courage.

Your reward? Alignment with that magical sense of harmony between your spiritual, emotional, and physical being - the *real you*.

When you're in harmony, you'll generate the perfect environment to cultivate *kaizen. Kaizen is a Japanese word meaning, to 'change for the better,'* - step-by- step improvements that transform our lives, day-by-day.

The Selfie of Truth

You already learned how to use *The Zen Button.*

It's time to introduce a second tool. What I call *The Selfie of Truth. The Selfie of Truth* empowers you to take a quick snapshot. To uncover what uplifts you and what holds you back.

Try this -

Set a timer. Just five minutes.

Allocate three minutes to write down five things you love about yourself.

Allocate two minutes - to jot down two things you know you need to change but won't admit to yourself.

Honesty is half the battle. That's it. You've taken a glimpse into your mirror of truth.

The Selfie of Truth is your emotional mirror. A pulse check on how closely your outer world aligns with your inner world. An easy way to measure your true inner happiness versus the *persona* you project to the world. Isn't it better to be who you are instead of who you pretend to be?

Your Seven-Day Transformation

You can experience *The Big Secret of HOW* in one of three ways:

OPTION 1: SEVEN-DAY DEEP DIVE

Dedicate yourself to *one part each day.* In just one week, you'll take seven bold steps towards your own version of *happy, meaningful success.*

OPTION 2: PERSONAL SELF - RETREAT

For a more intense experience, set aside a weekend and create your own retreat. Read, reflect, scribble down your thoughts - tuning in to you and your inner voice. Do it solo or with a friend, discussing insights, comparing notes and supporting each other.

OPTION 3: THE CHILL PILL APPROACH

No pressure. Take your time! Dip in whenever you need a five-minute breather - a pick-me-up, a calm reset.

This is your book. Use it the way that works for you - your pace, your energy.

And, as a nourishing bonus, after 30 years of being vegan, I'm including my recipe for what might just be the best hummus on the planet - perfect for snacking as you reach your destiny!

Are you ready to commit to your own personal workshop? What's not to like? Immerse yourself. Make time in your busy schedule. After all, when you feel like it, you find time to binge-watch Netflix late into the night, falling asleep halfway through the plot - so how about being the star in your own one-week transformation drama instead?

When you move from reflection to action, staying conscious of the life-force inside, you'll find:

A way to kick-start your inner transformation. To trigger a response that leads to positive change and inevitable transformation.

How to light up your unique path to meaningful success and to unlock the secret wisdom inside of you.

It's never too late. Meaningful success is *certain.*

Absolutely certain - if YOU want it enough.

Go for it!

Be Great Be Grateful

NOTES

PART ONE

POSITIVE MENTAL FITNESS
AND HAPPINESS

Rewire Your Brain for Success

POSITIVE MENTAL FITNESS
AND HAPPINESS

In Part One, we begin with a commentary on mental fitness, followed by a series of secrets - insights to shift your mindset and strengthen your inner life. These include how to change your life, find peace, stay mentally balanced, feel good about yourself, live free from fear, and how to conquer the mind - all without taking life too seriously. I'll also be asking questions for you to reflect on. As with each of the seven parts, to close, you'll read a short commentary reflecting on the key themes, followed by 'Motivation Zone' - a space offering tools to support you through life's challenges and turning points.

The Role of Reflection: Strengthening your Mental Fitness

Take a moment to reflect on all the achievements in your life so far. Don't diminish your well-earned victories. The small wins add up. Recognise the value in your progress as a stepping stone to your bigger goals.

It's easy to focus on what's missing, instead of appreciating what makes you already remarkable. But reflection alone isn't enough. Identify what's working for you and what's working against you. Mindful action unlocks the gold mine of hidden potential already inside.

The Hidden Cost of Suppressed Emotion is Stealing our Happiness

Have you ever wondered, "Why do I feel trapped, weighed down, and disconnected?" For many of us, this silent struggle is all too familiar.

It's easy to blame circumstances or others for our difficulties. However, what if the real reason we feel stuck isn't what's happening around us, but what we're holding inside?

Progress begins when we admit that our choices and actions are the root cause of our pain and suffering. Often buried deep within since childhood.

That's a bitter pill to swallow, but a truth worth exploring, no matter our discomfort.

We can mistakenly believe subconsciously that we are protecting ourselves by holding in our emotions, instead of releasing them. In fact, this *false* protection does the opposite. It increases our emotional burden.

By embracing this awareness, we can take charge of our emotional well-being. To let go of old patterns and release our emotions. The longer they are suppressed, the bigger the explosion.

The Science of Unhappiness

Suppressing our feelings isn't just uncomfortable - it's life-threatening. Read that again. Unhappiness makes us sick. A 12-year study published in the *Journal of Psychosomatic Research* found that people who suppress their emotions face a 35% higher risk of dying from any cause, and a 70% higher risk of dying from cancer. On top of that, we add further stress to our physical and mental health, often self-inflicted through unhealthy life choices.

The Power of Responsibility

It's not all doom and gloom! Here's the liberating truth. When we take full ownership of our difficulties, everything changes. Accepting responsibility for our emotional state is empowering and transformational.

Transformation doesn't need to be dramatic. It starts with small, conscious steps - a positive thought here, a kind word there. Each positive thought feeds and encourages the next positive thought. We become saturated with positivity. We rewire the brain. As Santiago Ramón y Cajal, the father of modern neuroscience, reminds us:

"Every man can, if he so desires, become the sculptor of his own brain." (Clearly Cajal meant this to be applied for all of us regardless of gender).

My Story: Breaking Old Patterns

Earlier, I asked you to pause and consider if you are happy and free. These questions might make you feel really uncomfortable. In the prologue, I shared how I spent years hiding my feelings, rarely stopping to check in with myself. For too long, without fully realising it, I covered up my emotions behind achievement and routine. Life had taught me to lock away my emotions, keeping everything inside.

At eight years old, I went to boarding school, where showing emotion was seen as a weakness. A reason to be teased or bullied. At home, feelings were never discussed. In my former marriage and relationships, I rarely expressed what I truly felt. At work, I wore a smile and soldiered on, pushing my feelings down, even when I was burnt out physically, mentally, and emotionally. *Get It Done* was my mantra. *GID*. I was driven to succeed, not realising that I was masking the *real me*. You might be in that place too.

I was living life on autopilot, disconnected from my feelings. The magic pill of meditation came just in time and helped me to survive.

It takes real courage and many *selfies of truth*, to break free from old patterns and let our guard down. To everyone who's ever said, "I'm fine," while struggling inside, this is your opportunity to start healing.

Here's an entry related to this topic from my 300 days of silence diary.

* * * SILENCE DIARY EXTRACT * * *

Day 106: Mindfulness in Silence

"When we are mindful, we realise happiness; when we forget, we lose touch with ourselves. The core of our being hides inside of us, waiting patiently. This silence is providing the key to the door to the crown jewels within - the home of untainted love, compassion, understanding and wisdom."

* * *

Your Turn: The Promise of Change

You have the power to sculpt your mind and your life.

The mind is like clay - mould it daily.

Break away from negative patterns, express your true self and build the life you deserve.

Start today. With each small step, you move closer to the life you deserve.

Positivity in Action

TRY THIS AFFIRMATION

Firstly, gently breathe in and out of the nostrils.

Anchor yourself in the flow of the moment.

Watch the life-force in each breath.

Sit straight.

Pay attention just above the eyebrows a little inside. Say out loud...

☆ I am the power of positivity.
☆ I choose to focus on what uplifts and empowers me.
☆ I feel *only* positivity.
☆ I stand by my decision to think with encouragement and hope.

☆   I am confident to speak my truth without fear.
☆   I commit to be guided by clarity and conscious decision making.

Affirmations are like loud music. Drowning out the doubts. Repeat daily. Aloud. Practise in front of the mirror before, during and after brushing your teeth. Let it become your new internal dialogue. A daily rhythm of belief.

Positivity in action creates the environment to express our true feelings to release and heal our hidden pain.

REFLECTION PROMPT

When was the last time you suppressed your feelings? How did it affect you? Take a moment to write them down or simply acknowledge your feelings.

Where and how can you release and express your feelings in a safe environment?

Who can you approach who will listen without judgement?

SECRET #1

HOW TO FIND HAPPINESS
before drowning your sorrows on a friday night

The secret wisdom whispers in your ear
Which thoughts do you hang out with the most?
Happy thoughts or unhappy thoughts?

What is a happy person?
A happy person is content alone or with others
A happy person feels blessed when trouble comes *because...*
...a happy person is grateful that their troubles are not far worse
...a happy person ignores the negatives of the mind
...is less reactive and more positively active

A happy person is relaxed - either when speaking or when in silence

A happy person smiles from the heart

What is an unhappy person?
An unhappy person is always in trouble
...finds fault in others and in themselves
...remembers the negatives of the past and projects negativity to the future
An unhappy person is negative - whether alone or with others
An unhappy person blames others for their problems...
...is an expert in misery

An unhappy person lives a life of unfulfillment

Do you spend more time in happiness or unhappiness?
Be honest
Pause for a moment
How often do you consciously choose happiness over unhappiness?

My friend, do not worry
The best answers come from the wisdom inside

We constantly oscillate between a state of happiness and unhappiness
We forget that happiness and unhappiness are tricks of the mind
We mistakenly associate happiness and unhappiness with a temporary, fleeting moment, thought or feeling

It's when we realise it's our own foolishness to waste power on...
...negative thoughts
...negative people
...negative events
It's when we realise it's our sole responsibility to make the mind our servant and not our master
It's when we realise these sparks of truth, we join the enlightened few who are on the path to contentment

When your body is in pain, it's "unhappy."
Stay calm, remain positive and detached

When your mind is restless, so what!
If someone insults you, so what!
If someone lets you down, so what!
If someone dislikes you, so what!
If you're having a bad day, so what!

Be the witness to your happiness and unhappiness

True happiness is being...
Being in consciousness
True unhappiness is *non-being...*
Non-being is a state of unconsciousness

Meditation brings inner happiness and contentment

Who Really Wants to Find Happiness?

MINDFUL THOUGHTS ON HAPPINESS

Instead of chasing happiness by getting hammered or sky-high on a Friday night;

Save your cash.

Go on a retreat with a bottle of Nozeco and a packet of crisps instead!

SECRET #2

HOW TO CHANGE YOUR LIFE
when you've run out of ideas

The secret wisdom whispers in your ear

To change ourselves is in our hands
To change our habits is in our hands
To change our life is in our hands

Our hands choose to light a cigarette or a candle of peace
Our hands choose to throw anti-depressants or healthy vitamins down our throats...
...to give to others or take from others
...to put too much food or alcohol in our mouths or just enough to stay content and healthy
Our hands choose to use money wisely or throw money away

The more we reinforce healthy habits, the easier it is to eradicate unhealthy habits
The more we embed unhealthy habits, the harder it is to cultivate healthy habits
The more we add good habits, the more we subtract bad habits
Small steps
Giant leaps

Good company makes us good
Bad company makes us bad

Blah blah, I hear you thinking!
Take responsibility, methinks!

What we do today is the result of yesterday
What we do tomorrow will be the result of today
What we did yesterday cannot be changed today

Are we conscious of truth in every thought, word and deed?
Are we conscious that we are the accumulation and
culmination of the past?
Are we conscious that it's never too late to change ourselves?

Meditation shows us what we need to change by tuning into
our Higher Power

Who Really Wants to Change Your Life?

MINDFUL THOUGHTS ON CHANGING YOUR LIFE

We all think, act and behave due to the past. Who we are
today has been influenced by our genes, conditioning and our
effort.

Broadly speaking: 20% genes, 30% conditioning and 50%
conscious effort.

You can't change your genes, the early teachings and influence
from your parents, teachers and friends. With effort, however,
you can change yourself.

Remember, if you work like crazy, you might come back next life as a donkey!

If you hate your job, change it.

If you always hate your job after switching over and over again, then maybe you need to change yourself.

When you change yourself, a new dynamic energy will surge from within and everyone will want to hire you.

SECRET #3

HOW TO FIND PEACE
when your mind is stressed

The secret wisdom whispers in your ear

If the mind is restless, we can never find peace
If the mind is restless, we can never find truth
If the mind is restless, we can never find our path

We will never find peace if our desires are endless...
...if our lives are consumed by constant worry
We will never find peace by ignoring our self-made reality

We can control our reactions and thoughts
We cannot control the reactions and thoughts of others
When we react, we give away our power and waste our energy
When we stay calm in adversity, we have mastered the mind's reaction

When we master the mind, we will find peace
When we master our diet and live within our means, we will find peace
When we truly love ourselves just as we are, we will find peace
When we accept others just as they are, we will find peace

Without love, there's no peace
Anger steals peace

Follow the motto, my friend:

"The past is dead, with your two eyes look straight ahead," - then nothing touches you

Be blessed with good memories
Be blessed with the ability to forget bad memories

Do you remember what you should forget or forget what you should remember?

It's a waste of time when you allow the mind to relive negative experiences
It's a waste of time to imagine a negative future when the future doesn't yet exist

Meditation is the tool to calm the breath...
...to calm the mind
...to unlock the door to inner peace
...to go to the space in between two thoughts
Meditation is the tool that unites us with inner bliss
It can't be forced

Contentment is the goal of life...
...the goal of the many
...the goal achieved by the few

Just Be

Who really wants peace?

MINDFUL THOUGHTS ON FINDING PEACE

To avoid a nervous breakdown, stare in the mirror for 45 minutes and imagine yourself running free in the forest without a care in the world.

As you begin to believe this is really you, then you will experience oneness and your *aha* moment. All your troubles will melt away.

If you no longer recognise yourself - call 999 and report an intruder in the house!

❧

What are your three big goals in life?

You can list them below:

1.

2.

3.

Are you having fun achieving these goals?

If yes, congratulations.

If not, consider adjusting your goals so you are happy today while achieving your goals of tomorrow.

❧

CONTEMPLATION CORNER

☆ Happiness ☆ Changing Your Life ☆ Peace ☆

I'm curious. Did you list happiness, changing yourself or being at peace, as one of your three big goals in life?

Here are some more questions you might like to consider.

Take a few minutes per question to write down your thoughts.

Be instinctive. Be spontaneous. Be truthful and reflective without self-criticism.

Turn your phone off. None of us is that important!

WHAT ARE YOU PREPARED TO DO IN THE NEXT WEEK TO MAKE YOUR LIFE HAPPIER?

WHAT POSITIVE CHANGES ARE YOU GOING TO MAKE WHICH WILL
DEFINITELY CHANGE THE WAY YOU THINK AND ACT?

WHAT ARE YOU COMMITTED TO CHANGE (UNDERWEAR EXCLUDED) TO
MAKE YOUR LIFE MORE PEACEFUL?

SECRET #4

HOW TO KEEP YOUR MIND BALANCED
when you don't have time to think

The secret wisdom whispers in your ear

What is the cause of an unbalanced mind?

The mind is an ocean of thoughts and ideas...
...a stream of positive and negative thoughts
The mind creates joy and misery...
...fear and unhappiness instead of courage and happiness
The mind is a bubbling pot of imagination
The mind is our taskmaster when it should be our servant

The mind focusses on what it wants - and we blindly follow
BUT
The mind is the key to set us free

What we eat affects the mind
What we drink affects the mind
What we see and hear influences the mind

To master the mind, meditate on the calmness in each breath
To master the mind...
...engage the mind with positive thoughts
...recognise when imagination is unhelpful
...take control

...instruct the mind firmly

...change your perspective

...ignore the negative thoughts in the monkey mind

A difficult day doesn't have to make the whole week difficult

A wonderful day might not make the whole week great, but you start tomorrow with a cheerful attitude

A balanced mind leads to a balanced life

A balanced mind helps you to manifest your dreams

A balanced mind leads to a happy mind

Who wants a balanced mind?

MINDFUL THOUGHTS ON KEEPING A BALANCED MIND

Strong likes and dislikes create imbalance. Be careful what you wish.

Create a powerful mental imbalance! 99% positive, 1% neutral.

If you want to check in with your true feelings, your attitude is the invisible marker that gives the snapshot of how you feel and if you are happy.

Consider what you are eating each day and if it suits your body and digestion. Some monks in Asia avoid garlic, onions or chilli, as these foods can make the mind restless and affect your meditation and sleep. If you can't sleep and love spicy food, try eating spicy food during the day, but not at night.

Consider for a moment, Leonardo Da Vinci's "Principles for the Development of a Complete Mind:

1) Study the science of art. 2) Study the art of science.
3) Develop your senses - especially learn how to see.
4) Realize that everything connects to everything else..."

Be Kind to Your Mind
BUT
Is Your Mind Kind to You?

SECRET #5

HOW TO LOOK GREAT
without having a facelift

The secret wisdom whispers in your ear

What's important?
To LOOK great or FEEL great?

Instead of thinking what we should wear to impress the crowd
Instead of thinking we should dress well for our partner
Instead of thinking what we wear defines us

Stop and think

Why do we allow others to define us?
Why do we care about what others think about us?
Why do we take so long to care about our body instead of our mind?

We look great when we realise greatness comes from inside...
...when our mind is still and our body healthy

Be great.
Be grateful.
Smile.
A smile wipes away 1,000 tears
It's your smile that lights up the world

As for clothes, dress for you
As for your smile, do you really smile enough?

As for how you look, the secret is to be yourself in all that you do

Meditation shows us that we are already absolutely perfect
Be Great and Meditate!

Who really wants to look great?

MINDFUL THOUGHTS ON LOOKING GREAT

According to Dr Michael Titze, a German psychologist, five-year-old children smile up to four hundred times every day. He explains that when we laugh, endorphins are produced in the brain that increase feelings of well-being and act as pain blockers. Laughter is good for reducing blood pressure and relaxing the muscles. By the time we are adults, smiling can reduce to fewer than fifteen times per day.

We come into the world crying and many of us will leave the world crying with regrets.

What about you? Will you leave the world smiling or crying?

Laughter is the only accessory that never goes out of fashion.

Save your cash. No Gucci clothes allowed in heaven. But if you must, at least make sure they're comfortable.

SECRET #6

HOW TO BE FREE FROM FEAR
whilst eating chocolate cake

The secret wisdom whispers in your ear

What is your biggest fear?
What is the cause of your fear?
What is the result of your fear?

Listen to these sobering words and smile
The biggest fear is death...
Death of the body
Death of the ego
Death of our loved ones...
...our career
...our mind

If we love today, fear dies today

The result of fear is doubts and worries...
The result of fear is negative thinking...

My sweet friend, contemplate deeply...
Are you living a miserable life in a state of *death* or an
exhilarating life in a state of *joy*?

Fear cannot survive in a climate of love
Fear cannot survive...
...when you see the best in every situation...

...when you appreciate all the positives of the day

...when you are confident and brimming with enthusiasm

Fear is so often caused by imagination...

In the darkest night, the rope in the grass might look like a snake, but it is a piece of rope!

Fear is caused by thinking the worst...

...instead of calmly thinking the best

Fear is caused by insecurity...

...instead of calmly creating a peaceful mind

Fear is caused by a lack of awareness...

...instead of calmly increasing your conscious thoughts

Fear is caused by a lack of optimism...

...instead of calmly being positive in every situation

Fear is caused by loneliness...

...instead of calmly being grateful for your family and friends

Fear is caused by anger and aggression...

...instead of calmly tapping into the peaceful Zen Master inside

Fear is caused by negative energy...

...negative thoughts

...negative words...

...instead of calmly being intelligent and staying positive

Fear is caused by imagination of separation...

...from our loved ones and

from our physical body

This body will go one day
This mind will be still one day...
...with a little luck, whilst we still have our marbles
When we defeat our fears...
our cells, atoms and molecules bounce up and down like a
moon party inside the body!

When we remove negativity, fear drops away
When we remove ourselves from negative situations, fear dies
away
Fear cannot survive when we are full of love

Be peaceful, my friend
Be joyful, my friend

Who wants to be free from fear?

MINDFUL THOUGHTS ABOUT BEING FREE FROM FEAR

The holy scripture from India, the Bhagavad Gita, 4:40, tells
us "A doubting person is always in trouble."

If death is your biggest fear, make life your biggest joy.

In case of emergency, instead of being afraid and miserable, eat
a huge slice of *Death-by-Chocolate* cake.

Smile in the mirror at your chocolate-covered lips!

Repeat as necessary.

Now you will be ready to face anything!

Did you know? In 2025, our biggest fear is losing our mobile phone. According to Direct Line Insurance, in the UK alone, an estimated two million people drop their phones down the toilet each year! If we multiply that statistic globally, it would equate to around two hundred million phones down the loo each year.

How about making your phobias fun?

Maybe you have something in common with the famous actress Tallulah Bankhead who said: "I have three phobias...I hate to go to bed, I hate to get up, and I hate to be alone!"

What are your funny phobias?

Nobody's looking.

Scribble away just for fun. Not everything in life has to have meaning.

SECRET #7

HOW TO CONQUER THE MIND
before eating bangers and mash

The secret wisdom whispers in your ear

When you conquer the mind, you master the thoughts
When you conquer the thoughts, you conquer life
When you conquer life, you transform blind faith into meaning and success

When you cultivate *meaningful success*, a tsunami of truth floods your mind
To conquer the mind, we have to conquer our beliefs

Positive beliefs are based on worthwhile imagination
...on conviction
...on optimistic visualisation
...on strength and courage
...on a series of successful actions
Our core beliefs are influenced by the positive and negative views of others

Ignore the negatives of the mind
Ignore the negatives inside
Ignore the lack of belief of others

Avoid people who put you down
Avoid people who have nothing good to say

My friend, we all have the potential to succeed in this world

Conquering the mind is the only victory worth winning

When a negative thought arrives, counter it with a positive thought

When a negative belief arrives, treat it as imagination and laugh loudly

When a negative person discourages you, be the witness and hold on to your beliefs

We are all going to be busy!

Faith is the catalyst for positive beliefs

Faith is the key to the door of success

Faith makes us; no faith breaks us

Who wants to conquer the mind?

MINDFUL THOUGHTS ON CONQUERING THE MIND

"Conquer the mind and you conquer the world." Guru Nanak, a 16th century sage from India.

When you feel a bit lost and lack belief, don't feel disheartened. Every successful person has doubt in their life.

Be bold. Don't take life too seriously.

Be a Swiftie for the day. Sing "Shake It Off." Move your hips.

Eat your favourite sizzling sausages with mashed potato and oodles of gravy.

CONTEMPLATION CORNER

☆ The Mind ☆ Looking Great ☆ Fear ☆

Positive mental fitness is a state of constant joyful awareness. A positive mind under our control leads to truth, meaning and purpose. What we pay attention to also becomes our reality. But....

WHAT DO WE DO WHEN WE'RE HAVING A BAD HAIR DAY?

How about laughing at ourselves? I didn't have a bad hair day for years - a quick polish does the job! Comedy is the food for the soul. Life is so often a dark comedy. Sometimes it's better to laugh than cry.

Here's a true story about me.

When I was born my mother's first words were, "I don't want a boy." My father laughed and said, "We can't put him back!" I had been rejected at birth. Quite literally after my first breath. When I learnt this at 25 years old, I was shocked and sad. When I think about it now, I just have to laugh.

WHAT DIFFICULT LIFE EXPERIENCE HAVE YOU OVERCOME THAT ONCE SEEMED OVERWHELMING BUT YOU NOW ACCEPT AS PART OF YOUR LIFE AND GROWTH?

HOW ABOUT JOTTING DOWN THREE THOUGHTS THAT MAKE YOU FEEL
DISILLUSIONED?

Now jot down six thoughts that make you smile. *Keep this list
handy. It's your emergency happiness kit.* When negative thoughts
come, smother them with an abundance of positive thoughts.

LOOKING AND FEELING GREAT

WHAT DO YOU LOVE ABOUT YOURSELF? SCRIBBLE AWAY FOR AS LONG
AS YOU LIKE. YOU'RE WORTH IT!

REFLECTIONS

Happiness

During my silence challenge, I became the silent witness to my happiness and unhappiness, my fears and doubts. When I felt miserable and alone, losing the ability to express myself verbally to friends or family was incredibly challenging. Yet it was also extremely rewarding. I learnt how to *be the witness,* when I realised that all thoughts come and go.

On my daily walks, I observed people going about their business. Wondering who was happy and who was unhappy.

Do you know who was the happiest person I saw every day?

A tramp who had nothing. A tramp who never begged. I nicknamed him Alfie. Alfie would lie on the same park bench every day, sunbathing with his feet up wearing his vest and underpants. Clothes folded neatly on the side. A beer in one hand, headphones on, listening to his favourite music. Smiling and singing to himself, he would stay there most days until dusk. Living with a smile, enjoying what he had in the present moment.

What can we learn about happiness from the man who had "nothing"?

We all want to know the secret to success and happiness. But maybe we are looking in the wrong direction. Are we plodding along today with blind hope of a happy tomorrow that may never come?

Are we focussing on the minutiae of life instead of the big picture?

Do we manifest daily what is good for us and defer what is bad for us indefinitely?

Is our happiness based on a temporary outside world of excitement that never lasts?

Can we just sit, smile and be content? Even sitting silently for 1% of the day - just 15 minutes, can positively impact our chaotic lives.

Lastly, are we giving and receiving unconditional love?

To be unconditionally loving all of the time would make us all saints. We can only do our best. When we fail, just try again.

To be happy and loving, we need to change our attitude

Our attitude determines who we attract, how we feel and react to ourselves and others.

Who is the 'Alfie' in your world? What can you learn from them?

When we treat every person like a VIP, our attitude transforms our careers, our lives and our emotional state of being. Try it and see for yourself. Notice what happens when you voice your opinions with a smile; order a coffee with a smile, or spontaneously help a stranger with a smile. Your warmth and kindness uplifts everyone around you.

We need to saturate our lives, minds and bodies with healthy habits.

How about jotting down three healthy dishes, three healthy drinks and three positive experiences you plan to have this week? See how it feels to cook an array of new dishes and concoct some healthy drinks.

Positive mental fitness sharpens the way we train and nourish the mind to the optimum for our maximum benefit. *Easy* or *difficult* become extinct and irrelevant. When we have a strong purpose, nothing can stop us.

A happy mind leads to a meaningful life.

Go For It!

MOTIVATION ZONE

Choose your *motivation and reflection moments* daily – when your day winds down or as the sun rises. The timing doesn't matter; what matters is making the effort.

From my silence, I observed...

Silence and stillness cannot be forced.

Stillness lets your mind enter a unique space, where reflection deepens and the seeds of change are quietly sown.

Silence is found in the secret space between two thoughts.

Treat this moment daily as a chance to renew your positive mental energy. To effortlessly dissolve negativity or fear. Carve out time each day to find a bit of calm – to check-in with the REAL YOU.

Step One

ACTIVATE *THE ZEN* BUTTON

There doesn't have to be a crisis to activate *The Zen Button*. Choose the same time each day for your Zen moment to build consistency.

Sit straight. Eyes open or closed. Conscious breathing. Watch the life-force carried by each breath. In and out of the nose. Detach from your thoughts with love. Witness every breath.

To dissipate negative thoughts and negative emotions, try focussing gently in the centre of the chest. This is the body's natural point of gravity. The place to anchor yourself and feel peace. The heart chakra. In the ancient Indian scriptures, the Upanishads, the heart chakra is referred to as the Seat of the Soul.

Be the witness. Be the passer-by without engaging in every drama.

You don't have to own every thought. Negative thoughts are not who you are. They're mostly temporary, fleeting and unimportant. Push them aside or just ignore them. Attention gives power. Why give away your power? Positivity is your true nature.

Keep good company inside. Is your mind a gold-mine of positivity or a nickel mine of negativity?

Adopt a *So What!* attitude. Negative thoughts only hurt you if you let them. Laugh at the drama of the mind. Like watching a bad movie - you soon forget about it. Do the same with your unwanted thoughts.

Think of them like a bounced-back email. *Return to sender. Address unknown.*

It's mostly imagination. How can imagination be real?

P.S. *So What!* is not supposed to be used as a defensive mechanism if someone hurts you. That's the time to sit with your feelings. Healing will come. If it's better to love someone from a distance, send them love mentally.

Memory recall. Remember three moments that made you happy today, no matter how small.

The Big Secret?

Ignore negative thoughts with loving detachment, as if they were never yours in the first place. That alone disempowers them. Try it and see.

Step Two

How You Are is How You Think

Thoughts reflect your mood, your attitude and feelings.

Check in with your mental fitness during the day.

Feeling tense or agitated after speaking with someone? Having a problem with a friend or a colleague? Step aside mentally. Don't carry it.

Take control of the moment so that it no longer has power over you. For example:

✦ You feel	Annoyed after a conversation.
✦ You think	*My opinions are dismissed and not respected.*
✦ Flip the Switch	*They're having a rough day or have problems I don't know about. I can speak to them later or tomorrow when my inner fire has calmed down. We don't have to agree on everything.*

The Big Secret

Inner conflict isn't inevitable. Outer conflict does not have to lead to inner conflict. Why react?

✦ Implant in your mind	*When differences arise, that's not a problem.*
✦ Remind yourself	*It's OK to agree to disagree.*
✦ Tell your mind	*I'm in charge now. You're on a tea-break until further notice.*

Step Three

Change Tactics

Try this approach.

Smile when you wake up and smile when you go to bed. That's not as easy as it sounds!

SELF-AUDIT: YOUR SELFIE OF TRUTH

Jot down...

What percentage of today were you happy?

What percentage of today were you unhappy?

Now reflect. Ask yourself.

Who is influencing me?

Who is in my circle?

Observe your next five calls or meetings with colleagues, friends and family.

Listen carefully.

Do you hear positivity or negativity? What's the ratio?

The results may shock you.

Develop meaningful friendships. Keep a healthy distance if you're being drained.

And last, but not least...

COMPARISON KILLS CONFIDENCE

Don't fall for the hype that others are better, smarter, or more successful than you. Nobody has it all figured out.

Remember, you're already fabulous. Own your fabulousness!

Count your blessings. Gratitude rewires the brain to see good everywhere.

Step Four

LOCK UP THE PEACE THIEF

Negativity and fear steal our peace and rob us of our happiness. Often in broad daylight! Each time you press *The Zen Button*, always anchor yourself in the flow of the moment. Create a calm moment to develop inner peace.

When Fear Knocks

Fear is a natural reaction to discomfort, but it's mostly imagination cloaked as danger.

A dog bites us when we are young. Fast forward to now. Every time a dog runs towards us, we panic. But it's just a memory reactivated - not reality. Past experiences do not have to repeat.

This is the mischievous power of the mind.

During my silent retreat, I started dreaming intensely with full memory of the dream when waking up.

Secret missions for the US president, playing professional football. You name it, I dreamt it!

On Day 17, I had a strange experience. A scary dream.

* * * SILENCE DIARY EXTRACT * * *

"Wake at 12.50 am, in a pool of sweat. In my dream, a witch calls me 'yogi'. I rarely have bad dreams. This one is so real. Cold shivers up the spine. Negative energy surrounds me. I pray for protection and remain detached. Be the witness, echoes in my head. I focus in the centre of the chest - the seat of the soul.

I push *The Zen Button* - hard! I'm not afraid. The witch, the fear - it's all inside of me."

THE MESSAGE?

I believe dreams carry messages. The message is clear.

I write the next morning on Day 18...

"Learn to accept everything equally - good and bad; love and fear. All experiences dissolve into nothing. Be the neutral witness.

A question arises. Should I close my heart to negative energies to protect myself? Will this disturb my meditation practice? If I open the door, will more come? I always feel protected so why protect against something 'bad' when it's part of me?"

And later the answer comes...

"Leave everything behind. It will pass. Don't stop. Keep the faith."

* * *

TRY THIS:

Write down what scares you.

Ask yourself: *Is my fear rational or irrational?*

Choose a fear and confront it. That doesn't mean running to the park to bite dogs!

Observe the fear without judgement. Seek reassurance from someone you trust.

Freedom from fear comes from...

Awareness:

Courage:

Compassionate action.

THE BIG SECRET?

Face your fears with love. Love conquers everything.

Thich Nhat Hanh, the famous Vietnamese monk, reminds us that fighting our fear is fighting ourselves. When we are afraid of our fear, we fear only our 'self'. The fear sits within us - suffering silently. If we push the fear, we compound our suffering. With mindful breathing, visualise that vulnerable part of us being held with love and recognition. He recommends we connect with the inner child inside.

Step Five

MOMENTUM MAKER FOR INNER PEACE

☆ There is no mind to conquer. Make your mind your best friend, and *the illusion* of the mind as an enemy will fade away.
☆ Love the mind. Love life.
☆ Seriously - don't take life too seriously!
☆ Trust yourself. The answer always arrives in the space between two thoughts.
☆ Align with the life-force in every breath and in every action.
☆ Be absorbed.

Accept What You Cannot Change

Resistance creates stress; acceptance opens the door to peace. Acceptance doesn't mean giving up - it's simply saying, *"This is how it is for now."*

Mind Mastery

Adjust expectations.

The biggest cause of restlessness is unfulfilled desires. The biggest cause of unhappiness is envy. Here's a challenge...

Create one quiet moment per day for the next seven days. Just five minutes. 300 seconds of calm. That's all.

In these calm moments, take time to reflect on what you already love about your life.

Final Thoughts

Uplift your thoughts.

Remember, even small steps count. If all you do this week is spend five minutes flooding the mind with positive thoughts, you're already making progress to be more peaceful.

Empower yourself! You've got this.

* * * SILENCE DIARY EXTRACT * * *

Day 112:

"Be the loving witness. Joy is everywhere.
Witness the joy inside and outside."

* * *

PART TWO

MEDITATION
MINDFULNESS & YOGA

Calm the Chaos Within

MEDITATION MINDFULNESS & YOGA

In Part Two, we begin with a commentary on going beyond the mind, followed by a series of secrets - insights to help you integrate meditation and short moments of silence into your life. These include how to calm the mind, to meditate, how to balance your energy, stay mindful, embrace silence and stay positive. I'll also be asking questions for you to reflect on. You'll then read a short section reflecting on the key themes, followed by 'Motivation Zone' - a space offering tools including powerful affirmations to steady the mind - especially when it misbehaves!

Beyond the Mind: Integrating Meditation, Mindfulness & Yoga into Daily Living

So far, we have experimented with *The Zen Button*, *The Selfie of Truth*, Positive Affirmations, *Flip the Switch*, *Being the Witness*, and adopting a *So What! Attitude*. These are simple yet effective tools to reflect and maintain your positive mental fitness, ensuring happiness remains the heartbeat of your life.

Part Two builds on that foundation - deepening your practice and broadening your understanding of meditation, mindfulness, yoga, and most importantly, yourself.

Remember - everything in *The Big Secret of HOW* is optional. You're free to take what resonates with you and discard the rest. But as you read, I suggest keeping *The Zen Button* pressed down at all times. It's a helpful reminder to stay open, mindful and receptive.

The Three Key Ingredients to Conscious Breathing

Integrate these three simple, conscious steps each day. To calm the mind and to concentrate longer than a goldfish, which manages nine seconds, compared to the human at eight seconds!

1) Breathe in and out through the nostrils, not the mouth;
2) Awareness of the life-force or *prana* (as described in India) or *Chi* (in the Far East) in every breath;
3) Focus either in the centre of the chest (the heart chakra) or just above the eyebrows (the third eye) a little inside, to activate the pituitary gland. See which area to focus, feels more natural for you. Focussing in the heart chakra develops more empathy and love; focussing in the third eye cultivates more wisdom.

Did You Know?

Scientific studies show that breathing in and out of the nostrils enhances oxygen intake, filters bacteria, promotes nitric oxide production (which aids blood circulation), and activates the parasympathetic nervous system, helping reduce stress.

The calmer the breath, the calmer the mind.

The Invisible Hand - Let's Talk About God

Here's the good news. Meditation, mindfulness, and yoga work for everyone, regardless of our religious or spiritual beliefs. Whether you're religious, atheist, or somewhere in between, it's about connection - to know ourselves, to have faith in ourselves and *TO JUST BE*.

When you integrate faith in your life, the magic happens. Faith destroys doubts. It doesn't matter if your faith is in yourself or your Higher Power - your positive energy is embedded into your self-development, whether that's through affirmations, meditation, or yoga. All empower you exponentially.

To find *happy, meaningful success*, you *have to believe* it's 110% possible - which is why your inner faith has a profound effect on your personal growth.

Personally, I'm not religious - hence the title of my first book - *The Invisible Hand: Business, Success & Spirituality*. But I feel a deep, inner connection to the teachings of numerous saints and sages whose words guide and inspire me. I experience God, not as a separate entity, but as the force that connects us all - a presence of love, peace, and wisdom that can be felt in stillness. How I see God maybe helps you too. In short. God is Love and Love is God.

Hidden Paths: Mysticism in Religion

Every major religion has its mystical side, often hidden from mainstream view. These practices - whether meditation, prayer, or physical movement (such as yoga) - share a common thread: stillness, introspection, and the pursuit of connection with a higher power.

For example:

✧ CHRISTIANITY	Hesychasm (Greek for stillness and silence) and Christian mysticism, which emphasises direct experience with God through prayer and breath awareness.
✧ ISLAM	Sufism - focusing on love and spiritual simplicity.
✧ JUDAISM	Kabbalah - seeking divine wisdom.
✧ HINDUISM	Yoga (union with the Self through meditation and mindfulness), Vedanta (the end of knowledge), and Bhakti (devotion).

✧ BUDDHISM	Zen - concentration and direct experience.
✧ INDIGENOUS CULTURES	Shamanism - healing and spiritual connection.

What's Meditation?

Ask ten people to describe meditation, mindfulness and yoga and you'll get ten different answers. Ask why they stopped practising and you'll hear the same answers -

I couldn't stop my thoughts, so it didn't work for me.
I don't have time. My meditation is walking or golf.
And, my favourite - *I'm too stressed to meditate.*

Maybe you're in this category too.

I'm always surprised how quickly people give up. The rewards of meditation are life-changing, but the *many* stop after a few attempts. Ironically, the busiest people, who have the least time, often end up making meditation a daily habit after experiencing just a brief moment of calm.

Reflect for a moment.

Did you try meditation and then give up?

Do you give up easily in different areas of your life?

Do you believe that your mind is busier than when you started to practise meditation?

When we meditate, we become aware of the mental noise that's always been inside. Don't let that discourage you. Keep going.

My Story: Stop Fidgeting

It took me five years of daily practice (between 15-30 minutes a day) to make meditation as natural as brushing my teeth. Even when working 70-hour weeks or waking up at 4 a.m. to meditate before a three-hour drive to a meeting, I made time for meditation.

There were weeks and sometimes months, where I couldn't sit still for 20 minutes without my mind going into overdrive. I would move my body, get distracted by a stray fly, or feel an itch that needed scratching. But I stuck with it, applying my favourite *So What* attitude.

The Art of Balance - Yoga

Meditating daily may sound like a big challenge for you. I encourage you to keep going.

My daily practice is Kriya Yoga, an authentic meditation technique, as taught to Gandhi and Mother Teresa. Many people are attracted to Kriya Yoga through the famous book *An Autobiography of a Yogi*. This book was the favourite of Steve Jobs who ensured that every person who attended his funeral received a copy.

This ancient practice combines physical postures (*asanas*), breathing exercises, and meditation to maintain constant awareness of *prana* (life-force energy). Kriya Yoga is the essence of the four main paths of yoga:

✧ RAJA YOGA   The path of meditation.

✧ KARMA YOGA   Conscious awareness in every thought and action.

✧ JNANI YOGA   The pursuit of wisdom.

✧ BHAKTI YOGA   Devotion and service to the world.

Yoga helps us to integrate these paths into daily life. It's not just about postures and breath work - it's about paying attention to the energy being moved through the mind and body by the breath. Choose a yoga that works for you and enjoy it!

Mindfulness

Mindfulness and meditation are like the two wings of a bird. Both need each other.

Alone they cannot operate efficiently, in the same way a plane can't fly properly with one engine down.

Mindfulness develops through stillness. The end product of meditation.

Mindfulness is a state of pure being. Pure receptiveness to this moment in time.

Being calmly present in the flow of the moment leads us to three states.

1. Total absorption in the present moment.
2. Non-judgmental observation.
3. Acceptance of whatever is happening right now.

Meditation without mindfulness is like cleaning a frying pan that gets dirty again moments later, without understanding why it needed cleaning in the first place. You feel better for a while, but without mindful awareness throughout the day, you slip straight back into the same unhelpful habits.

Mindfulness without meditation is like knowing the pan needs cleaning, but you refuse to pick up the sponge and washing up liquid! Mindfulness develops concentration. Mindfulness *without* meditation can inadvertently make you become even 'better' at concentrating on your negative thoughts!

Your Turn: The Promise of Change

You've made it this far, so you're already taking great strides - keep going!

How about committing to read the next chapters with *The Zen Button* pressed down?

REFLECTION PROMPT

* * * SILENCE DIARY EXTRACT * * *

Thought of the day. Day 32: "Do I have enough faith?"

* * *

Take a moment to pause and reflect.

How do you feel in silence?

How about committing to just one minute of gratefulness in silence before tonight's dinner?

SECRET #8

HOW TO CALM THE MIND
even if you can't sit still

The secret wisdom whispers in your ear

If we want to calm the mind, we need to calm our lives
If we want to calm our lives, we need to calm the mind
To calm the mind, we need to calm the breath
To calm the breath, we need to calm our desires

When we calm our desires, we find balance
When we find balance, our breath becomes calm
When we find calmness, we find happiness

Meditation calms our breath
Meditation calms our minds
Meditation calms our lives
Meditation calms our desires

Who really wants to calm the mind?

MINDFUL THOUGHTS ON HOW TO CALM THE MIND

Scream at the mirror instead of shouting at your partner, your
phone or the kids.

To develop patience, call your bank's helpline.
If that doesn't work, try meditation, not medication!

Calm Breath = Calm Mind
Restless Breath = Restless Mind

Reset Moment
Pre-set a calm alert on your
phone three times per day
Close your eyes for sixty seconds
Stay in the flow of the moment
with every conscious breath
Feeling calmer?

SECRET #9

HOW TO MEDITATE
without chanting om

The secret wisdom whispers in your ear

Meditation is the key to calmness and happiness...
...the sweetest fruit to sample daily...
...the path to wisdom and stillness
Meditation is for everyone including the busiest people
Meditation is the source of endless energy to help you achieve success

I hear you say...
"My mind is busy"
"I don't have time"
"It doesn't work for me"
"I don't even pray"

My friend, don't be discouraged
Don't give up

How long does it take a baby to learn how to walk and talk?
How long does it take to learn a new language?
How long does it take to be independent?

To become an expert in our field takes time, patience and strength
We are all beginners on the path of truth
So, here's a perfect way to get you started each day:

Shut the eight doors including your eyes
What are the eight doors? I hear you ask!

The door to the room is the first door
Next, you have to 'close' the seven *doors* in the body to switch
off the five senses
Your eyes
Your ears
Your nostrils
Your mouth

Open the window a little for fresh air
Ok, open your eyes to do this
Don't jump!

Turn off your phone
The world will still be spinning without you

Set the alarm for five minutes
Sit straight with your chin a fraction down
Rest your hands on your legs, palms facing upwards
Close your eyes gently
Keep your spine straight
Witness the breath finding its rhythm in and out of the nose
Conscious breathing

Relaxed focus in the centre of the chest
Watch the breath there
Be still
Breathe gently in and out of the nose, not the mouth
Gentle breath

Relax...

...no hurry, hot curry!

...witness the gentle flow of the breath

...slowly more calmness will come

...no need to control your mind or your breath

...be the smiling, silent witness

If the focus drifts away, just gently return to watching each breath in the centre of the chest

Sit silently

Meditate

Stop thinking about what you're having for dinner

Relax

Five minutes of meditation can feel like running a marathon

Congratulations! You are now an accomplished yogi

The secret is to be one with the powerful energy within each breath

...to watch the breath and not the mind

...to watch the life-force in each breath

...to ignore and let go of the thoughts during meditation

...to ignore and let go of the negative thoughts outside of meditation

The secret is to practise daily...

...to be the silent witness

...to go beyond the mind, body and senses

Who wants to meditate?

MINDFUL THOUGHTS ON MEDITATION

Meditation is the superfood for the mind.

Meditation is a state of perception not hallucination.

Meditation is the silent fuel that can empower you each day.

Isn't it true? You always find time for what you want to do - no matter how busy your life.

If you find time for your bad habits, you can also make time for your good habits.

Increase your meditation from five minutes to fifteen minutes a day when you feel ready.

Fifteen minutes of meditation is just 1% of your day. Keep the other 99%.

That's nine hundred vital seconds to recharge and rebalance your energy.

In return, you gain more calmness in the day. Meditation could turn out to be the best investment you ever made.

Try it and see. After three months, evaluate. *What is your change?*

MEANINGFUL PROMPT

How do you feel when you're still?

ACTION PROMPT

Try meditating in the morning or evening. See which suits you best. It's advisable to meditate before food, but not after food. Stick to the same time each day.

C-ALMNESS	*Conquers*	ALL
A-NGER	*Destroys*	EVERYTHING
L-OVE	*Brings*	MAGIC
M-EDITATION	*Creates*	CALMNESS

SECRET #10

HOW TO BALANCE YOUR ENERGY
chakras explained - no need to hug a crystal

The secret wisdom whispers in your ear

What is a chakra, my friend?

We cannot see a chakra, so why should we believe chakras even exist?

Chakras are mentioned in the Vedas, the sacred texts of India, written over 10,000 years ago

Chakras are discussed in yogic and tantric texts such as the Upanishads

Chakras are described as energy centres in the body, along the spine to the top of the head

Chakras are focal points in most forms of meditation

...including Buddhism and Hinduism

When we meditate, we gain calmness more easily by focussing on the chakras

A chakra is a concentrated flow of invisible energy

A chakra out of balance exposes our weaknesses

A chakra in balance manifests our strengths

A chakra is the invisible magnet for the source of life and all activity

My friend, here's some mumbo-jumbo in Sanskrit on the main seven chakras...

The first chakra, Muladhara chakra, also known as the Root chakra, is located at the bottom of the spine:

Earth is the corresponding element; smell is the corresponding sense

Physical strength, survival, success and failure are influenced here

The second chakra, Svadhisthana chakra, also known as the Sacral chakra, is located just behind the sexual organs:

Water is the corresponding element; Taste is the corresponding sense

Friendships, family, sexual relations are influenced here

The third chakra, Manipura chakra, also known as the Solar Plexus chakra, is located just behind the belly button:

Fire is the corresponding element; Sight is the corresponding sense

Digestive power - what we consume and drink, are influenced here

What we eat and drink affects the mind

The fourth chakra, Anahata chakra, also known as the Heart chakra, is located in the centre of the chest

Air is the corresponding element; Touch is the corresponding sense

Our emotions and expression of love and fear emanate from here

Too much emotion brings us trouble; too little emotion brings us trouble

The fifth chakra, Vishuddha chakra, also known as the Throat chakra, is located in the throat area

Space is the corresponding element; Sound is the corresponding sense

How we speak, express ourselves and our beliefs emanate from here

If we look at our lives...

...we can see what is balanced

...we can see what is unbalanced

...we can see what can be changed

The sixth chakra, Ajna chakra, also known as the Third Eye chakra, is located in the centre of the forehead

This is the powerhouse which attracts the life-force

The seventh chakra, Sahasrara chakra, also known as the Crown chakra, is located at the top of the head

The Crown chakra is the magnet for stillness, power, love and peace

To balance our lives, it helps to meditate

Meditation automatically catalyses balance

When we meditate...

...we withdraw our thoughts from the external world to the inner world

...we focus gently on each chakra, feeling the pure energy in each breath

...we go beyond the five senses

When we meditate deeply, the mind withdraws from the five lower chakras to the two higher chakras

Believe nothing, my friend

Try it and see for yourself

Experience trumps second-hand knowledge and beliefs
Experience develops with time and practice
Experience brings practical knowledge and our own
transformation

Who wants more balance?

MINDFUL THOUGHTS ON BALANCING YOUR ENERGY

According to the great Sage Vashista:

13 seconds of meditation, has the same auspiciousness as
giving away a valuable possession to charity.

101 seconds of meditation gives the same merit as performing
a sacred rite.

12 minutes of meditation multiplies the merit 1,000-fold.

By setting aside just 12 minutes to meditate each day, we are
rewarded with 12,000 minutes of evolution

The good news is every teacher was once a student and every
saint was once a sinner.

There's hope yet for all of us.

Try This

Focus for one minute in the heart chakra. Send love and
kindness to three people who need it right now.

SECRET #11

HOW TO BREATHE
like a god and not a dog

The secret wisdom whispers in your ear

Brothers and sisters, do not fear

It's not necessary to wait for a happy new year
You can change your life here and now

Every inhalation is life
Every exhalation, a temporary death
Every inhalation is a new beginning
Every exhalation, a temporary end

Every breath is a chance to live a healthy lifestyle
...an opportunity for growth
Every breath in calmness is a positive breath
Every breath in anger and agitation is a wasted breath

Yogis breathe in and out of the nose
Yogis breathe like gods and not dogs
Yogis never strain the body or mind

Consider following these ancient yogic practices to optimise
your health...
Keep the stomach half empty
Keep the stomach one quarter full of water
Keep the stomach one quarter full of food

Yogic breath is calm, rhythmic and gentle

It energises the body and quietens the mind

Yogic practices can also help the body look beautiful

BUT

Yogic practices have been created to make the mind even more beautiful

To remain fit and healthy, exercise and stretch at least 30 minutes each day in fresh air

To remain mentally fit, stay conscious of the gentle power in each breath

This gentle power is known as *prana*

Stay conscious of the *prana* carried by each breath during our daily activities

Never miss a day of being conscious

Build a daily routine of physical exercise, stretching, yoga and Pilates

Who really wants to breathe like a god?

MINDFUL THOUGHTS ON BREATHING LIKE A GOD AND NOT A DOG

There are numerous breathing techniques.

Breathing techniques for meditation are designed to make the breath calmer to bring you to a state of stillness.

When you meditate deeply, your breath becomes still and the mind becomes still.

Special yogic techniques (*pranayama*) oxygenate the body and mind.

As a reminder, *Prana* means life-force, known also (as I said earlier) as *chi* or *qi* in Tai Chi and martial arts.

Pranayama is the movement of *prana* through the breath and the chakras, energising the body.

Keep going. Stillness is guaranteed.

Meditation might just be the driver to take you to your magic moment of stillness - when life begins to make sense and any doubts fade away far into the sunset.

*Meditation Unlocks the
Door to The Unlimited Mind
Feel free to give it a go*

SECRET #12

HOW TO PRACTISE YOGA TO RESET THE MIND
without wearing lycra

The secret wisdom whispers in your ear

Do we practise yoga to look great or feel great?

Yoga has thirty-two meanings in Sanskrit
Including...
Friendship. Union. Doing Business. Even being a spy!

Yoga is an art, a science and a way of life
Yoga is the catalyst for learning and burning...
Learning what is good for us
Burning what is bad for us

Yoga manifests....
...calmness in the mind
...peace in our body
...love towards our fellow living beings

Yoga activates union...
...to unite with our true nature
...to unite with calmness, peacefulness and happiness

THE BIG SECRET of yoga postures is to prepare the body and mind for meditation
Meditation and yoga are soul mates
Yoga offers a way to explore meaning and values

The great sage Patanjali, breaks down Yoga into eight constituent parts

Yama is the practice to control the restless mind and body

Asana is the practice of how to find the correct position of the body

Niyama is the way to follow the path of duty

Pranayama is the breathing practice of how to expand our energy and purify the mind and body

Pratyahara is the path to withdraw the senses through stilling the mind

Dharana is the path to concentration to achieve our noble goals and peace

Dhyana is the pathway to profound meditation

Samadhi is the eighth category...

Samadhi is the result of sincere practice of the first seven categories
...the fulfilment of life
...the ultimate goal of freedom
...the constant state of balance
...and liberation

Who really wants to practise yoga?

MINDFUL THOUGHTS
ON YOGA TO RESET THE MIND

"Yoga is excellence in action." Bhagavad Gita 2:50

Not feeling it? No stress. Be relaxed.

After your yoga class, do your best to be serene and peaceful.

Sip organic sencha green tea.

Eat a dried-out vegan energy ball with a spirulina smoothie.

Book yourself on a raw cacao ceremony.

Splash out on an expensive yoga mat to complete your path to yoga mastery.

Stillness = Awareness
Awareness = Clarity

CONTEMPLATION CORNER

☆ Calmness ☆ Meditation ☆ Yoga ☆ Breath ☆

Meditation takes us to the calm place. The place few of us visit on a daily basis. In meditation we visit our personal cocoon. Impregnable to negativity. When the breath is still, the mind is still. This is my direct experience of meditation and yoga. There's everything to gain and nothing to lose. What's not to like?

THE BIG SECRET to meditation is to ignore the mind and focus on the pure energy in each breath.

Many successful people meditate. Oprah Winfrey, Lady Gaga, Sir Paul McCartney, Michael Jordan, Erling Haaland, Novak Djokovic, Arianna Huffington and Steven Bartlett, to name just a few...if it works for them, surely it can work for you.

HOW ABOUT COMMITTING TO 10-15 MINUTES OF MEDITATION EVERY DAY FOR THE NEXT WEEK?

WANT TO TRY YOGA? FIND A CLASS AND TRY IT OUT.

WHAT POSITIVE STEPS ARE YOU PREPARED TO TAKE TO BECOME A BETTER PERSON?

QUICK MIND CHECK
Is your mind dominated by
the 'F' word or the 'C' word?
Turn to the next page to find out!

Which words come to mind?

Faith and Consciousness perhaps? Your state of mind is the key to happiness and success.

Now give yourself an HONEST score:

0 to +5 on each word beginning with the letter 'C' below

0 to -5 on each word beginning with the letter 'F' below

(+5 being the highest and -5 the lowest.)

+'s	-'s
Courage	Fear
Calmness	Freneticism
Compassion	Fragility
Confidence	Foolishness
Cheerfulness	Failure
Consciousness	Falsehood
Creativity	Frustration

TOTAL +'s   =   [   ]

TOTAL -'s   =   [   ]

GRAND TOTAL =   [   ]

Subtract your -'s from your +'s. If you score +35, you're already a superstar! If you score -35, things can only get better!

SECRET #13

HOW TO BE MINDFUL IN DAILY LIFE
when you're too busy to breathe

The secret wisdom whispers in your ear

To be mindful is to be full of *calmness* and *clarity*...

...to be free from all unnecessary thoughts

To be mindful is to expand our practice of kindness at home and at work...

...to take care of others

A cynic might observe that mindful people...

...aren't always happy people

...contemplate their navels until the sun goes down

...might have the certificates, but are not always calm and happy

Theory and practice, my friend, theory and practice

None of us is perfect

Mindfulness really works

Mindful people practise...

...controlling their senses...

...controlling their reactions

...how to defuse an argument by listening rather than shouting

...how to really care about others

Mindful people are conscious, positive people

Mindful people meditate daily and correct themselves frequently

Mindful people disrupt the inner environment that breeds negativity

To be mindful is innate in every human being

To live in the evolving milliseconds of now

Our state of mindfulness is the cumulative result and application of our daily yoga and meditation practice

Who wants to be mindful?

MINDFUL THOUGHTS
ON HOW TO BE MINDFUL IN DAILY LIFE

According to the National Science Foundation, 80% of our thoughts are negative and 95% are repetitive.

Ignore your negative thoughts.

Pay attention to your positive thoughts.

Be mindful...

Support your local hospital by *not* turning up, because you're fit and healthy.

Support a charity that needs your money or your time and not a charity which invests in stocks and shares.

ACTION TIME: Offer to help a friend this week - mindfully, selflessly, without any result in mind.

DID YOU KNOW? Mindfulness can shrink your amygdala (the brain's fear centre) and boost your immune system.

* * * SILENCE DIARY EXTRACT * * *

Day 109 - "Silence whispers the truth."

* * *

SECRET #14

HOW TO SURVIVE A DAY IN SILENCE
without going stir crazy

The secret wisdom whispers in your ear

Silence is manna from heaven...
...the manna of beauty
...the manna of the humble
...the manna of purposeful energy
...the manna of the seeker
Silence is the soothing manna for the mind

To spend a day in silence means
No distractions
No internet
No phone
No music
No TV
No social media
No speaking
No laziness

Are those your footsteps I hear running for the door?
...running towards the noise?
...running to the nearest Wi-Fi point?

The thought of silence scares the restless many
and smiles to the calm few

The thought of silence ringing in our ears sends us into panic mode

The silent mind is the perfected mind
...the inventive mind
...the calmest mind
The silent mind speaks truth beyond the cacophony of thoughts

Silence is the greatest mastery
Try it and see
New is neither hard nor easy
Just New!
Close your mouth
Open your mind
Open your heart
Ignore your thoughts

Who wants to survive a day in silence?

MINDFUL THOUGHTS ON SILENCE

"Truth is the offspring of silence and meditation." Isaac Newton.

Don't panic - you don't have to do a day's silence or 300 days! Start with five minutes per day.

Sit relaxed, eyes open, enjoying the moment, in nature and fresh air.

Visualise that you are a great Buddha sitting silently.

A chosen few of us are already blessed with Buddha bellies and no hair on our heads!

Really do visualise yourself as a great Buddha!

Developing your Buddha nature starts with belief and silence.

ACTION TIME

Eat one meal this week in silence without your phone or outside distractions. Notice the flavours, textures and thoughts that arise.

DID YOU KNOW?

Scientists tell us that even short periods of silence can boost creativity and reduce stress.

❁

* * * SILENCE DIARY EXTRACT * * *

Day 34: "The voiceless sound of silence sings to me."

* * *

❁

SECRET #15

HOW TO STAY POSITIVE
when surrounded by negativity

The secret wisdom whispers in your ear

Positive people never give up...
...they see rejection and failure as small steps towards success
...they see the best qualities in everyone
And make the best of every situation

Negative people spend time with negative people
Negative people seek solace and sympathy from anyone who will listen...
...feed off the negative experiences of others
...enjoy talking constantly about their problems and the problems of others

My friend
Look inside
None of us is 100% positive
None of us is 100% negative
BUT
When we look deeply at our life...
...at what we think
...at what we say
Are we positive or negative?

The truth inside never lies

Do we surround ourselves with positive or negative friends?
...with positive or negative work colleagues?
...with positive or negative family members?
Are we attracting positive or negative people?

Stop to think for a moment or two
What is my truth?

All of us have positive and negative experiences
All of us have the power to be positive or the choice to be negative
The power to choose our friends and where we work
Are we more influenced by negativity or positivity?

Always be positive about life...
...about what you see
...about what you hear
...about what you say
I agree with you if you're thinking...
"It's easier said than done"
Be compassionate to yourself
Nothing worthwhile happens overnight
Inner peace does not just arrive the following morning

THE BIG SECRET is to...
Celebrate every small success and laugh at every small failure
Surround yourself with positive people
Be positive when life isn't going your way

Who wants positivity?

MINDFUL THOUGHTS ON STAYING POSITIVE

If you're feeling down, don't lose hope. Change your mood. Do or read something positive.

Positive means even just a smile when you don't feel like smiling.

The smallest positive action creates wave after wave of positive reactions.

Add a new, positive habit each week...

Negative habits and thoughts will no longer be the centre of attention.

If negative friends surround you, then change your friends.

If you want a better job, be brave and go for it!

I'M CURIOUS

Who is the most positive person you know? What's their secret?

Feeling low or a bit sorry for yourself today?
Don't lose hope
Play "Levels" by Avicii
Dance your socks off!

CONTEMPLATION CORNER

☆ Mindfulness ☆ Silence ☆ Positivity ☆

It's easy to waste time on our problems and negatives, instead of having gratitude for our blessings and positives.

Self-analysis is not another opportunity to moan about life

Transforming our attitude by becoming the mindful witness to events and consciously ignoring harmful thoughts is active positive mental fitness. Self-analysis is a wonderful chance to be honest and manifest miracles in our lives.

We know we are ready to change…

…when we reach breaking point or when we intuitively trust that change is the only path ahead.

Have no doubt. Meditation creates a state of active calmness. When you're proactive, calm and put in the effort, change has no choice but to come. The most effective change is when you are contemplative and mindful about your choices.

As you scribble down your wholehearted truth, be loving to yourself. Eat a snack to keep you company. My go-to-nosh is dark organic chocolate. *What's yours?*

When we spend 90% of our mental energy and focus on our positives and mindfully eradicate our negatives, the world and our minds become a better place.

WRITE DOWN THREE POSITIVE AFFIRMATIONS (REMINDING YOURSELF
HOW MARVELLOUS YOU ARE) TO USE WHEN YOU FEEL A BIT DOWN IN
THE DUMPS

Practise being silent, especially when you're feeling angry or
negative towards others

Anger poisons the mind, the body and emotions. Sit silently for
five minutes today. Do nothing else. Just Be. Try it and see.

What habits are you going to change? How about making
the mindful choice to focus on just your positive thoughts?
Mindfulness and meditation are like twins. Both bring
harmony when practised in our daily lives.

Pain	→	Suffering
Suffering	→	Surrender
Surrender	→	Realization
Realization	→	Change
Change	→	Happiness

REFLECTIONS

Embracing Agitation - Insights From a Retreat

Once I was on a meditation retreat. I sat down to meditate, but people were talking and laughing outside my room. I was agitated. *This is supposed to be a place to meditate*, I thought.

I decided to go to a quieter part of the property. I found a room, closed my eyes but two minutes later someone came in. The room was needed for a meeting. Agitated again, I went to the main meditation room. Relief. Surely I would find peace here. Within minutes, the hedge-cutter outside was in overdrive. I smiled and remained there. After a while, the noise bothered me less until I didn't notice it any more. Finally, the hedge-cutting stopped. But by then, the silence had already arrived inside.

It was a lesson in life ...

Not to be so easily distracted by outside influences and not to give away my power.

Whether it's the noise of a hedge-cutter or the chatter of the mind, THE BIG SECRET of finding *happy, meaningful success* is to continue regardless of the distractions. Meditation teaches us to be detached without reacting, to allow thoughts to come and go.

Monkey Mind - The Struggle to Find Stillness

External noise isn't the only distraction. Sometimes, even in silence, the mind is racing. Another time, I was organising a yoga event. A friend of mine, Luisa, could sit perfectly cross-legged on the floor, unlike me - I always sits in a chair. She had practised yoga and meditation for years. She didn't move her body once. After the programme, Luisa came up to me and asked how she could still her mind, as it was so restless! I was surprised. She had found a way to sit completely still in spite of her restless mind.

The mind is always busy, it's the nature of the mind. But the goal of meditation is not to force the mind to stop, but to go beyond the mind. Observe it without judgement and allow it to settle over time.

Natural Thoughts During Meditation

Don't Panic! Every kind of thought comes to us in meditation. You're in good company. Thoughts come thick and fast that do their utmost to put us off! Guess what? No problem at all. Let them come. Continue. Smile. Ignore. *So What!*

Meditation is not about silencing the mind; it's about accepting whatever arises and returning your attention to the life-force in each breath. In time, your mind will thank you and look forward to meditation.

Here's a typical list of thoughts that can come to mind during meditation. Feel free to add your own too!

1. I need the loo.
2. My mind is super busy today.
3. What's for dinner?
4. My phone hasn't rung.
5. This silence is scary.
6. Can't the neighbours stop arguing? I'm meditating.
7. I forgot to feed the dog.
8. What's happening at the weekend?
9. Shall I skip work on Friday to take a long weekend?
10. 15 minutes of meditation seems like an eternity.

It's normal for the mind to be busy and for the mental chatter to persist. THE BIG SECRET is not to engage with the thoughts, but simply to let them come and go. Over time, this practice helps you find calm and clarity in the chaos of daily life. So, when your mind runs wild, please remember, don't judge it, observe it and then let it go. And keep going. With patience, the stillness inside will come.

Why Persistence Matters in Meditation

Most people understandably ask if meditation will help them be less stressed, less angry or less reactive.

I can say from my personal experience the answer is YES! As we discussed earlier, people give up because they think meditation doesn't work if the mind is running amok in different directions. The mind's always been busy! In time it will calm down. Let it be. My mind may still kick in even now, but it doesn't bother me. Why do we pay so much attention to the mind and the thoughts?

We've become so used to living as human *doings* that we forget how to simply *be,* not just as human beings, but as divine beings! Meditation is a state of being. Mindfulness is a state of *being* in every movement, physical, emotional and mental. Yoga is a state of union - a way to live in harmony.

Find a meditation technique that suits you. Keep going. If a non-believer like me could benefit so much during my stressful career, so can you.

You've got this. *Go For It!*

MOTIVATION ZONE

The Power of Affirmations

In between meditation, mindfulness and yoga, we've already practised affirmations.

Where do affirmations come from?

Émile Coué, the famous psychiatrist, helped popularise affirmations in modern times, showing that positive affirmations reshape our minds. He described affirmations as 'medicine for the mind.' For example, 'Every day, in every way, I'm getting better and better.' Saints and sages from India created mantras thousands of years ago for success, health and prosperity. The Sanskrit word *mantra* means *to protect, liberate and calm the mind.*

The great Kriya Yoga master, Paramahamsa Yogananda, teaches that repeating affirmations with conviction, removes negativity, retrains the mind and awakens our highest potential.

TRY THIS AFFIRMATION:

The Breath of the Self

1. Gently breathe in and out through the nose.
2. Anchor yourself in the flow of the moment.
3. Watch the life-force in each breath.
4. Sit straight.
5. Bring your attention to the space just above the eyebrows. Look inside.

Repeat each affirmation gently out loud as often as you like.

Let each affirmation echo gently through your breath

Feel the breath resonate through your mind, body and spirit.

Let your body speak it. Let your being become it.

☆ **I AM ONE WITH THE UNIVERSE**
Feel your connection with energy, intelligence, and infinite space.
Silence and awareness - all merged together in your body, in every breath.
The life-force is energising every breath you take.
This is not just oxygen - it's the energy of life moving in each breath.

☆ **I AM PURE CONSCIOUSNESS**
Feel each cell, atom, and molecule within you.
You are not a separate being - you are absorbed in awareness.
You are stillness and movement.

☆ **I AM THAT**
Timeless, formless, and yet with form.
This is the state of being where the seer, the sight, and the seen are one.
Full connection with everything.
Take your time. No hurry before reading more.

Wait a Minute!

If I had read this in my late twenties, I would have laughed. Feel free to laugh along too! I've changed because I have experienced how positive universal words empower us. How does it feel for you?

Is Your Mind Your Enemy or Your Friend?

How often do you let the voice in your head convince you that you are small, unworthy and distant from others?

The mind can spin illusions, but the life-force in each breath brings you home.

You are not your doubts. You are not your fears.

Be the witness. That's all.

TRY THIS:

✧ YOU FEEL	Unhappy and lack confidence.
✧ YOU THINK	*These thoughts are real*
✧ FLIP THE SWITCH	*These thoughts will pass and don't define me. The prana in each breath reminds me that I am connected with love and kindness everywhere. I am not the doubts and fears of the mind. I have the power to choose peace and happiness instead.*

The Vital Life-Force

Scientists teach that we are made up of cells, atoms and molecules. Energy and electric activity. We cannot see with our eyes if what they tell us is true, but we believe it without seeing any proof. Saints and sages from all religions directly or indirectly tell us that we are held together by a life-force. Should we believe or disbelieve them?

For example...

Prana or Shakti (Hinduism and Yogic practices) - Divine energy.

Chi or Qi (Buddhism, Taoism and Eastern philosophies) - The energy that flows through the universe.

Ruh (Sufism) - The soul - the divine spark.

Ruach Elohim (Kabbalah and The Old Testament) - The breath of God.

According to these philosophies, what we breathe is more than air and oxygen. It's consciousness moving through every breath.

Each conscious inhalation carries love, power and intelligence. Each exhalation releases negativity, weakness and resistance. Let the *prana* flow.

A Suggestion

Feel free to use the words *My Higher Power, God, Universe, Mother Earth, Buddha,* even *Love,* as the connector between you and your universal power - or pick any word that resonates with your spiritual beliefs. Whatever motivates you the most. For example, as a positive mental exercise to find calmness, be conscious that your *Higher Power* is breathing; or God is doing everything; or the Universe is holding you with love and compassion. It's also a positive way to end the day before falling asleep.

Lastly, some practitioners count the number of breaths or affirmations during meditation. Our true essence reveals itself when we simply allow ourselves to be present without being distracted. Your mind might tell you "I need to count," or "I need music" before you meditate, but that's just the mind keeping control and subconsciously forming a long-term habit. Up to you, but it's an amazing feeling when the mind becomes totally still with silence all around.

The goal is to disengage and quieten the mind, not to let it dictate to us. When we release the habit of counting or the need for background music, we create the space for stillness and a deeper connection with ourselves.

Meditation - Don't Wait for Perfection

Consistency is the key that drives success in all that we do. I would rather you sit down for 15 minutes each day than attend a ten-day Vipassana retreat and then hardly meditate again. Small daily commitments in all that we do, always yield more lasting results than short bursts of intense enthusiasm.

Every time you sit down to meditate, you're doing something positive for yourself, even if it feels like your mind is running around in every direction. Keep going. Each moment of meditation builds on the last. If someone like me can find peace through meditation, so can you.

If your mind is full of excuses today try this:

✧ You feel   I don't have time to meditate today.

✧ You think   *I'll do it tomorrow.*

✧ Flip the Switch   *Just 15 minutes of meditation will set up my day perfectly. I will feel energised, positive and productive after meditation.*

Take note of what Gandhi said. When he had a packed day ahead, he said, "I have so much to do today, instead of one hour of meditation, I will meditate for two hours!

You've got this – take the leap and go for it!

❦

"Relaxation is the path to infinity."
Paramahamsa Yogananda

PART THREE

LOVE SELF-LOVE & FAMILY

Build Relationships that Matter

LOVE SELF-LOVE & FAMILY

In Part Three, we discuss love, followed by more secrets - an opportunity to reflect about our relationships, family, faith and the importance of loving ourselves unconditionally. I also reveal some of my deeper experiences from my time in silence and more big questions for you to consider. You'll then read a short commentary on the key themes, followed by 'Motivation Zone' - a space offering tools to help manage your thoughts when life isn't always going to plan.

Now that you've calmed the mind, it's time to open your heart.

This is where connection begins - with yourself, your loved ones and the world.

How Deep is Your Love?

In yogic philosophy, it is taught that on the right-hand side of the brain sit the negative qualities - anger, pride, cruelty, selfishness, insincerity and unhappiness. On the left-hand side of the brain sit the positive qualities of love, faith, kindness, sweetness, humility and happiness. We all have unlimited access to these traits. When we meditate, we bring more love and balance to our lives - diminishing the power of our negative qualities and increasing the power and influence of our positive qualities.

As you've come this far, you're already thinking deeply about what makes you feel good in your life - how to think and be more positive, how to feel more love for yourself and towards others and to take more control of who you are and who you want to be.

How much time do you spend thinking about love or any lack of love, instead of being present with the essence of love that is already inside and around you already?

My Story - Thoughts about Love During 300 Days of Silence

During my silence, I had many thoughts about love, family and relationships. I'm now going to share with you a glimpse of my feelings and thoughts about love from my time in silence. They are real, unfiltered reflections, not some abstract ideas.

Perhaps some of these reflections will resonate with you or spark your own thoughts and experiences about love - how you give and receive love.

* * * SILENCE DIARY EXTRACTS * * *

Day 33: Conditional Love and Expectations

"When we are unhappy, who is unhappy? If it's just the mind or body then who are we really? When we say we love someone, is it only when they do something pleasant for us or because we are physically attracted to them? Are we conditional in relationships and love? If we expect love from others we are so often met with disappointment. *Contemplation mode is in overdrive this morning.* I remember once an old girlfriend showing me her diary. I was taken aback - all about unfulfilled desires, unreachable goals and her huge disappointments in love and life. No doubt after our relationship ended, I was added to the list!"

* * *

Day 34: Struggling With Self-Love

"Internal dialogue on how to love more. *This love comes deep from inside. Mine is just not strong enough. I feel helpless.* I cry.

My mind says deep love will never come. I put a stop to that thought. It will come when it's ready. Negativity must be discarded."

* * *

Day 51: Uncovering My True Nature

"What has happened is a decoupling inside. Beyond the mind and body. Is it the soul I am experiencing? The true nature within is surely being uncovered layer by layer - through the life-force in each breath - still and loving."

* * *

Day 55: Family Dynamics

"I think of my upbringing. My dad sacrificed a lot for myself and my siblings. Yet it's a family trait that we find it easier to express the negatives instead of the positives. A silent disapproval lurks beneath the surface from parents to children. It's painful, but ultimately we can only change ourselves not others.

I guess it's rare to find parents that can listen to and accept their children with love and understanding. How many parents tell their children that they love them unconditionally? Certainly not in my circle of friends. Hardly any of us have parents who stop for a second to contemplate the impact of their decisions, especially as a result of their own relationships *and* the impact of their decisions on us their children."

[I don't even remember writing all this down. Fascinating how these topics continue in families, and so often without healthy resolution.]

* * *

Day 80: Experiencing Unconditional Love

"Something has broken. The secret entrance is open, allowing me to feel more love from *IT* - the indescribable God. I feel separated from mind and body. Both mind and body are relaxed - awaiting my instructions. How strange it feels. Normally they instruct me and I react. I am feeling *IT's* embrace internally. Warmth - encompassing - love - togetherness - gentle - liberating - stillness. So, this is love. No fireworks. It just is - *and* I didn't do anything. Unconditional love has presented itself. *IT* wants nothing from me and I offer nothing in return. I have entered unfamiliar territory. A new deep experience of love without effort. Unconditional love from the true place inside."

* * *

Day 102: All You Need is Love

"There's a wedding at the castle where I am staying. 'All You Need Is Love' bellows out from the speakers. I can smell cigarette smoke coming into the flat from every angle. This would normally bother me. I hear the sounds of a boisterous crowd, from the local football terraces a few miles down the road. 'All together now.' I like it. I'm not disturbed. Love really *is* all you need, whether in silence or on your wedding day."

* * *

Day 114: Becoming the Love We Seek

"Am thinking about love. We have to become the love we want to see in the world. Do we see love everywhere or always what's wrong?"

* * *

Day 156: The Freedom of Love

"Thought of the Day: *When love flows with every breath, all struggles cease to exist.*"

* * *

Day 183: Love Reveals Truth

"Thought of the Day: *Love without effort reveals the powerful truth.*"

* * *

Day 280: Self-Acceptance

"Love is to accept and love myself and others. Not to be afraid of failure and loss. My life and who I spend time with must be conducive to my spiritual practice. *Am I growing spiritually? Am I becoming more loving? Am I learning? Am I becoming a better person? Am I improving?* It doesn't always feel like it but I hope so!"

* * *

Exploring Love - The Heart of Connection

I discovered in silence that true love is waiting inside of us. What does love look like for you? Feel free to pause and close your eyes to *feel* your answer coming from inside.

What are you thinking? How are you feeling? Perhaps you're thinking of a special person who you love now or a loved one who is no longer with you. You might be thinking about what makes you happy in the world. Your family, your house, holidays, nights out with friends or nature. It could be anything. But are you really content and living a life of love, or hoping to find love and contentment one day soon?

Your Turn - Take a Selfie of Truth

Take a quick non critical, non-judgemental look at your feelings. How's the barometer of love in your life?

Amazing, Great, Good, Ok, Below Average, Awful, or No Comment?

Family Love Barometer ?

Friends' Love Barometer?

Partner's Love Barometer?

REFLECTION PROMPT

What can you change about your life to attract more love? You don't have to answer now. Put it on the back burner. Keep reading. Stay open.

SECRET #16

HOW TO ATTRACT YOUR IDEAL PARTNER
without swiping forever

The secret wisdom whispers in your ear

Do we attract what we want or what we imagine we want?

Do we attract what we deserve, or do we think we deserve much more?

Do we attract exactly who we are supposed to attract?

We attract love if we love...

...fear if we fear

We attract negative people if we are negative...

...positive people if we are positive

Our actions, our emotions, our thoughts...

All create...

...attraction, reaction and distraction

To find our ideal partner is a mysterious journey

To find any partner is an exhausting journey!

To find our perfect partner, try something new...

Audaces fortuna juvat...

...fortune favours the brave...

Talk to strangers

Strangers are all potential best friends and partners

Be mindful even when shopping

Carpe diem!

Approach a friendly-looking stranger who's not wearing a wedding ring!

Ask casually for top tips on the best way to cook wild mushroom risotto

Then with a smile, ask when your potential partner is free to taste your risotto

Laugh at both success and failure

If you do not try, you will never succeed

We know we have found our ideal partner when......

Our cooking is so bad, our partner tells us it's the best meal of their life

Our snoring is so loud our partner tells us they had the best night sleep ever after being awake all night

Our house is so untidy our partner smiles as they trip over our clothes all over the house

We know we have found love when......

We are loved for who we are and not who our partner wants us to be

We love and accept our partner just as they are and not who we want them to be

We love and trust our partner with our secrets

without fear of judgement

We are loved and trusted by our partner

without fear or embarrassment

We smile and laugh at our partner's bad habits

We smile and laugh because our partner accepts our bad habits!

We smile and know deep down our partner is our best friend

Who really wants to attract their ideal partner?

MINDFUL THOUGHTS ON ATTRACTING YOUR IDEAL PARTNER

Walk into a crowded room.

Talk to strangers and make eye contact; your phone is not your lover.

Make your move and remember to smile with confidence as you splutter out the words, "Are you free for a Babycham?"

MEANINGFUL PROMPT

If you had to pitch yourself on a dating show, what would be your opening line?

FACT NOT FICTION

There's a recent trend in Spain where singles congregate between 7-8pm at Mercadona supermarket. If you place a pineapple upside-down in your trolley it means you're single and looking for love.

SECRET #17

HOW TO BRING MORE LOVE INTO YOUR LIFE
without appearing on love island

The secret wisdom whispers in your ear

We spend our life searching for love

We spend our life...

...loving others who may not love us

...pleasing others who may not please us

...being loving and kind to others when they are not loving
and kind to us

...searching for love from a person who probably doesn't exist

....hoping others will love us the way we want to be loved

We hear so often that life is...

...about love

...about loving ourselves

...about loving our neighbour

We hear so often about loving...

...our partner

...our family

...about loving everyone

Are we searching for love outside when the real love is inside?

Do we blame others when we are the true cause of our
disappointments and failures?

Are we spending our time expecting that those we love will love us one day?

What is the truth of love, my friend?

Think deeply
Stay calm
Take a soothing, conscious breath
Open your heart

The secret wisdom understands the love you want
Love is unfathomable - so hard to grasp, understand and find
Pause
Think
Feel your truth
Say out loud each question below slowly

Can we love others if we do not love ourselves?
Can we love others who hurt us?
Can we love others who do not love us?
Can we love others who disagree with us?
Can we love more than one lover or must we choose?

Do we love unconditionally or is our love just a needy, selfish love?

Expectation in love leads to success or disappointment
...to joy or regret
...to happiness or unhappiness

Love is the potion we seek the most...
...the potion that softens our hearts

...the potion that melts away all doubt and fear

Love is the hardest word to say
Love is the hardest invisible friend to find and keep

My friend, don't be sad if the adventure of love doesn't always go to plan
Stay confident and positive

You are loved!
The secret wisdom loves you just as you are...
...unconditionally
The secret wisdom loves and understands you
The secret wisdom loves your smile and laughter
and loves you even when you are unhappy

Who do you want to tell "I love you"?
Why do you search for love when the secret wisdom inside loves you already?

Who wants to bring more love into their life?

MINDFUL THOUGHTS ON LOVE

It's always tough when you love someone more than they love you.
If your partner dumps you for someone younger, richer and more attractive than you
REPEAT 100 times..."I'm amazing, invincible and a great catch."

If your partner dumps you for someone older, poorer and less attractive than you,

REPEAT 1,000 times..."I'm amazing, invincible and a great catch."

Wipe away your tears. Save the planet. Use fewer tissues.

Remember this book is about not taking life too seriously!

JUST FOR FUN

Write down an unusual place you met someone you dated.

ASK is the Turkish word for love
AST is the Icelandic word for love
Be careful calling a stranger an ASS
If they come from Iceland or Türkiye they might think you are in love with them.

CONTEMPLATION CORNER

☆ Love & Relationships ☆

We all need love. We all want to be loved. We all want our love to be accepted. But do we truly accept and love ourselves just as we are? We need to love ourselves first before we can give and receive love more deeply.

WHAT ARE YOU PREPARED TO IMPROVE AND CHANGE ABOUT YOURSELF TODAY TO BECOME A BETTER PARTNER? You might need a few years on this question. You're not allowed to leave the room until you answer!

TO ATTRACT YOUR PERFECT DREAM PARTNER, WHAT DO YOU HAVE TO OFFER TO BE THEIR DREAM PARTNER?

WHAT QUALITIES DO YOUR BEST FRIENDS HAVE THAT YOU WOULD LIKE TO ADD TO YOUR AMAZING PERSONALITY?

Keep reading...this is a handbook for all moments...asking some of life's BIG QUESTIONS so you can find your own BIG ANSWERS. Sometimes we don't know whether to give up or keep going. Don't give yourself a hard time if you slip up now and again. The secret wisdom is with you every step of the way.

The next *Secret* is about Family.

Family stuff can be heavy duty.

Keep *The Zen Button* firmly pressed down!

SECRET #18

HOW TO STAY CONNECTED WITH YOUR FAMILY
without the drama

The secret wisdom whispers in your ear

Destiny creates family
Family creates destiny
Family teaches us our likes and dislikes
Family teaches us about love

Family love can be based on true love and acceptance...
...or expectations and conformity
Family love can break our hearts if it's conditional or non-existent
Family love or lack of family love affects us the whole of our life
...it influences how we express love to others
Family love can only be in balance if the family is balanced
Family love is based on the state of the family mindset
The truth for many is not so sweet
Many of us come from dysfunctional families

We bury the emotional burden and trauma from our childhood
We feel underappreciated and undervalued
We can have disappointing relationships with our parents and siblings

So, what can you do?

FIND yourself and BE yourself
Ditch the habit to meet the controlling expectations of others

Live a life of courage
Live a life that you want and not what your family expects
Live a life of love and kindness as best you can
Live a life of *ahimsa**, not harming your fellow living beings
If you cannot be near your family, love them from afar
If you cannot speak to your family, stay open for another day
If you cannot get along with them, ask yourself - am I being
kind and compassionate?

If you can, resist burning bridges
However hard it may be, keep the family door open -
something good may come
Let go of expectation
Free yourself from disappointment

If you long for family love, start by loving yourself
Don't blame your family for the way they are - you are part of
them
...you are responsible for yourself
Don't blame your family for the lack of love in your life - you
are the source of infinite love

Don't despair
From darkness comes light

Who wants to stay connected with their family?

MINDFUL THOUGHTS ON FAMILY

Whether we like it or not, we are the product of our family. None of us can change the opening chapter of our lives. Our parents or siblings are part of it, regardless of our relationship today.

We *can, however,* change our attitude.

If your relationship with your family is difficult, perhaps acknowledge that you are part of the problem and part of the solution.

Contemplate the value of negative thinking and criticism towards your family as well as what they project towards you.

Close your eyes for a few minutes daily. Send positive thoughts to family members or old friends where conflict exists. Focus on their positive qualities.

As a former cynic, I can understand completely why this may sound like a worthless and meaningless exercise. BUT when you contemplate the huge power of negativity on your feelings and others, this can be reversed by acknowledging the far greater power of positivity, especially on your mind and emotions.

If the family door to love is closed, make your close friends your family.

Lastly and most importantly, go towards the welcoming door of love wherever that may be.

Love moves where it is needed the most.

Ahimsa is the Sanskrit word for non-violence and peace. Gandhi described *ahimsa* as being our highest duty in life - to refrain from violence and stay peaceful.

Meaningful prompt

You're verbally abused directly by a family member. Unprovoked. Stand your ground. Say your truth. If they can't hear your truth, remove yourself. Let time pass.

Tune into your feelings. Is your love still the same as it was before the fallout?

Write down the positive qualities of the family member.

MESSAGE TO ALL PARENTS

We will remember your loving words and critical words for the rest of our lives.

Tell us often, from the depth of your heart, *no matter* how old we are:

"I LOVE you."

"I am PROUD of you."

"I really CARE for you."

"I have every CONFIDENCE in you."

"I have no doubt that you will find the WAY to succeed in whatever you want."

"I am GRATEFUL to you."

"I am HERE for you."

"You are a BEAUTIFUL person inside and out."

Is that so hard?

SECRET #19

HOW TO INCREASE YOUR FAITH
when the chips are down

The secret wisdom whispers in your ear

From darkness comes light
From darkness your hidden strength reveals itself
From the darkest moments something good always comes

Is there a person without problems in the world?
...who has not suffered?
...who has not faced shock, pain and adversity?

Have faith, my friend
The secret wisdom has faith in YOU!
Smile and have faith in YOURSELF...
...in your ability
...in the universe which protects and guides you

No more tears

Have faith in the brilliant person that you are
...in the courage and determination inside of you
...and know that your humble efforts will be rewarded

Nobody has 100% faith
Be great and have 110% faith
Nobody has faith every moment
Be bold and be faithful to yourself

Nobody with faith hasn't fallen

Be great and stand tall
Be courageous and banish all fear

Who wants more faith?

MINDFUL THOUGHTS ON INCREASING YOUR FAITH

Some of us have faith in God.
For me, as mentioned earlier, God is another word for love.
That's all.
If you don't believe in God, HAVE FAITH in LOVE.

"The smallest seed of faith is better than the largest fruit of happiness." - Henry David Thoreau, a 19th century American philosopher.

"There is a crack, a crack in everything.
That's how the light gets in."
Leonard Cohen,
famous song writer and performer

SECRET #20

HOW TO LOVE YOURSELF UNCONDITIONALLY
without being a narcissist

The secret wisdom whispers in your ear

The secret wisdom has already told you, "I love you."
Stop searching for love that looks like love but isn't love

True love is unconditional
True love requires no effort...
...comes from deep within
...is there all the time, just waiting
True love is nourishing and kind
True love is bliss

Why look outside for love when true love comes from YOU?
Why react with anger and fear instead of love and kindness?

Love is already here
Love is your silent friend who never leaves you
Love is holding you together even if you forget it

Be brave!
Love unconditionally
Love others just as they are
Manifest love in every breath

Who wants to love themselves unconditionally?

MINDFUL THOUGHTS ON
LOVING YOURSELF UNCONDITIONALLY

When you are feeling low, meditate quietly, focussing on the heart chakra in the centre of the chest.

The chakra of love and compassion. The seat of meditation.

Feel the stillness in every inhalation.

Feel the power in each silent breath.

Feel the love in every thought and breath.

Value yourself. Respect yourself.

Healthy inner love attracts nourishing love around you.

Two minutes later, as a reward, munch on your favourite cookies to show extra big love for yourself.

L-IVE A LIFE *of* MEANING
O-NENESS *with* ALL
V-IRTUE *in every* ACTION
E-GO *left* BEHIND

CONTEMPLATION CORNER

☆ Family ☆ Faith ☆ Love ☆

A life of love is a happy life, a life of laughter, a worthwhile life.

To live a life of love starts with us and our attitude. To love, we have to cultivate gratitude, forgiveness and humility. When we help others, these qualities multiply.

WHAT DO YOU LOVE ABOUT YOUR FAMILY? TAKE TEN MINUTES

WHAT DO YOU DISLIKE ABOUT YOUR FAMILY? TAKE ONE MINUTE!

HOW HAS YOUR FAITH (IN YOURSELF) OR OTHERS HELPED YOU IN YOUR LIFE?

Love = Kindness
Kindness = Compassion

REFLECTIONS

Love & Understanding

I shared earlier in the book about my mother rejecting me at birth. I didn't do this to make you feel sorry for me or to moan about life. Instead to show that every one of us has difficulties and sometimes the only medicine is laughter.

Only in recent years, I found out that in the first five years of her life, my mother was moved from house to house, hidden in fear during the Second World War. Sadly, she did not see her father after her childhood. My mother had mental health and addiction issues. Once I discovered more about her background, it gave me much more understanding. To imagine her constant fear, it gave me more empathy and more love for her even if I didn't see her very much after childhood.

When we tune into another person's pain and suffering, instead of our own, we can develop more love and understanding.

Love Hurts

It's extremely easy to sugar-coat love and life. Theory and practice are distant cousins when it comes to love. The fullness of life ensures that we will all experience happiness and sadness. We have no choice but to embrace every experience, like it or not.

Love brings joy and beautiful experiences which inevitably are followed by sadness, disappointment, loss and grief. Love in relationships is more often than not messy, complicated and a commotion of emotions.

When we aren't loved, we all want to know why. There's nothing worse than being rejected and not loved. Somehow, those closest to us have the automatic knack of hurting us the most, even with a few words.

The more we are attached, the more open we are, the more vulnerable we become.

If we apply yogic philosophy to our lives, an important lesson is to be *detached with love* in everything we do. To enjoy every moment but to realise that every moment, good or bad, will pass. Guruji, a humble Kriya Yoga master in India, often reminds us, "Life is a little sweet and sour, we are to taste it."

The big question is whether we keep a mental diary of love and joy or what we *expect* life to give us?

Consider for a moment whether you are loving to yourself and to others? *Sometimes but not always* is my answer.

To change your patterns, you have no choice but to change your attitude. Wise people enjoy the happy moments. Discontented people see what's wrong and can't enjoy the moment. They always choose to be pessimistic. I have an amazing friend called Kofi in LA. If you ask how he is, he always says the same. "I'm celebrating life." Not just words. He means it.

It's down to us. True love is far more than enjoying an external, temporary experience. Inner love acts as a barometer to our outer manifestation of love.

Strong inner faith leads us to love and gratitude.

Be kind and loving to yourself. Repeat kindness often.

Remember the words of Snoopy. "It's ok if some people dislike you. Not everyone has good taste!" *Go For It!*

Feel free to keep choosing what's right for you and good for you...

Self-analysis and self-reflection are solo journeys. Your own positive thoughts have dynamic power. Your dynamic energy will become a beacon of light, illuminating your very own path to *happy, meaningful success* that lasts.

The secret wisdom has absolute faith in YOU!

MOTIVATION ZONE

Love Starts with You

To be open is to be vulnerable, that's why we avoid showing our true feelings. How many of us are taught that showing vulnerability is a strength? Instead, we bury our feelings or defend ourselves and sometimes resort to *attack* as the best form of defence. THE BIG SECRET to find love, which leads to *happy, meaningful success*, is to firstly heal our pain and suffering and then to find our true inner love inside. I'm happy to admit freely to you that I'm a *Work in Progress* when it comes to love. What I do know, is that emotional cowardice doesn't serve us well and nor does anger when we are frustrated.

If I slip up, I forgive myself. I suggest you do the same. Reset, centre yourself in the flow of the moment and try again.

I've learned that in the right environment, there's a real freedom in facing what blocks our ability to fully love and be loved. Life has a canny way of forcing us to face ourselves. A turn of events, disagreements, what's hiding under the carpet must come up.

I have also realised that meditation on its own just isn't enough. Being truly in the beauty of the present moment - beyond emotions, mind and body - only happens, when we have started to untie the emotional knots within us.

Consciousness is the Cure to All of Your Suffering

Becoming aware of the patterns that hold us back is half the journey.

The other half? Self-acceptance.

According to Carl Rogers, the influential psychologist who introduced Client Centred Therapy, self-acceptance, is the #1 predictor of happiness. He taught that distress arises when there's a gap between our *self-concept* (how we see ourselves now) versus the *ideal self* (who we think we should be). The smaller the gap, the more the two are aligned, the greater our sense of well-being.

Love Letters From Sedona

Once I stayed in an Airbnb with a yoga teacher in Sedona.

On Miss Sedona's mantelpiece was a beautiful hand-written card. It was signed off *Love from your Darling*. It was gushing, full of love and full of compliments. When I asked how long she had been with her amazing partner, she told me she didn't have a partner. I was taken aback. Miss Sedona had written it to herself after attending a course to manifest her dream man.

Anything positive that helps our self-esteem and confidence is powerful, but projecting and imagining our *ideal self* and *ideal partner* might misguide us into thinking that the universe will take care of everything. The universe is inside of us, so we need to take care of our inner universe if we want someone to be attracted to us.

Visualisation and manifestation techniques are an excellent tool to prepare us for different outcomes and to rewire and activate the brain. However, if we visualise our dream partner but ignore the inner work needed to make ourselves a great catch, then we risk disappointment when our perfect partner doesn't magically appear at our door.

Here are some examples on how to change your thinking on difficult topics.

✧ You feel — Lonely and discouraged.

✧ You tell yourself — *I'll never find someone who loves and understands me.*

✧FLIP THE SWITCH

I'm working on building a kind, honest and loving relationship with myself. There's no rush. The happier I am, the more likely I will attract a partner who reflects that same positive energy, so we can both grow together.

TAKE ACTION

Once a week treat yourself to a *date* with nature. Reflect, walk, sit, journal and just enjoy the beauty of your surroundings. Take a moment for self-compassion. Write down three qualities you appreciate and love about yourself. Remind yourself daily. Don't forget to munch on your favourite snack.

TACKLING UNHAPPINESS

✧ YOU FEEL

Insecure or unhappy about yourself and your relationships.

✧ YOU TELL YOURSELF

I'm not good enough for a relationship and my family criticises me and puts me down.

✧ FLIP THE SWITCH

I'm worthy of love and respect from myself and others. Any criticism or disapproval does not define my value or truth.

I now choose...

...to set healthy boundaries with people who put me down.

...to build stronger, more supportive connections.

...to approach the open doors of love around me, rather than the closed doors where I expect love to be present.

I choose to focus on growth not perfection.

I'm proud of myself for having the courage to no longer give away my power.

Take action

Pause for a moment to reflect on the many acts of kindness and love you have shown others. When you're ready, have a calm, honest conversation with your partner or family member. Express yourself without judgment or blame. If that's not possible, reach out to a trusted friend. Stay grounded. Express yourself without slipping into *poor me* mode!

Remember - Relationships are a two-way street. Invest time to reflect on your own behaviour too. Are there patterns and reactions you're ready to release that do not serve you well?

Your reflections

This part of the book is deeply personal. You'll realise by now I see humour as an essential ingredient to nurture communication, healing and love.

Jot down how you are feeling about yourself right now.

Notice what's positive and what's negative - reflect, smile, move on.

Try This - *Create your very own positive affirmation*

You can call it *The Breath of Love.*
Centre your affirmations on self-love and self-acceptance. Be authentic. Trust yourself. Allow the breath to create inner peace and love.

1)

2)

3)

You've got this! You really do.

PART FOUR

PURPOSE
WISDOM & FREEDOM

Discover your Unique Path

PURPOSE WISDOM & FREEDOM

In Part Four, we open with a commentary about my bond trading days, followed by more secrets - to help tap into your wisdom to find meaning, staying true to yourself and exploring what makes a great leader. You'll read further questions in Contemplation Corner and then suggestions on how to quit habits that do not serve us well. Lastly, we return to 'Motivation Zone' - your private space to find ways to reclaim your power and take back control.

By now, you're already pondering over the questions you know need answering. The ones that keep you up at night and the ones that get you jumping out of bed in the morning. And more importantly, you're beginning to uncover the answers. However, sometimes, the more we try or the harder we think, the more we hit a dead end! Don't worry. This is a natural process, albeit an annoying one! Keep the faith. Something amazing is coming for you.

My Story

ANSWERS ALWAYS COME WHEN WE LEAST EXPECT THEM

When I was a bond trader in the City, one morning I found myself at the station, suited and booted on the platform at 6:05 am, thinking ahead to the traders' meeting at 7am. I suddenly realised I was the only one there. I waited ten minutes, thinking *"the train is late or am I?"* No mobile phones back then. I wondered if my watch was wrong. Then it hit me. *"It's Saturday."* I'd lost all sense of time and self-care. Sometimes I'd get calls at night from New York or Hong Kong, so I was always on alert, remembering my overnight positions in the market. Standing there alone on the platform, I knew this job could never be for the long term. I was losing all sense of reality. I gave myself a good telling off, all the way to the local café for an early bird English fry up!

The Silence Revelation - When Stillness Reveals the True Path

Finding your purpose doesn't happen overnight. It's a gradual and revealing process. I used to hate anybody telling me to be patient, so I'm reluctant to do the same to you, but *be patient* even once a week! Sincere desire and enthusiasm will guide you.

* * * SILENCE DIARY EXTRACT * * *

On Day 235 of my silence, a profound realisation reveals itself from the core of my being. "Purpose isn't something we find - it emerges when we become still enough to listen to our own inner wisdom. It appears when we remove the distractions - when the noise of the mind and the chaos of the world ceases to exist - because we no longer respond to them. In that special moment, we discover our true purpose and realisation - that there is no separation between the material and spiritual world. Everything is spiritual. Then we find our true purpose and meaning - simply, to exist and co-exist with love in our hearts. When we are in this state of *being,* we find joy in all that we do."

* * *

I can really understand if you feel that my silence experience is far away from your day-to-day reality. I was in the same boat when I started to meditate. At 34, I met Baba, the 91-year-old guru who changed my life. He spent 12 years in silence. I bombarded him with questions about spirituality.

One day, I asked him, "What is the purpose of life?" He replied, "You are *only* born for self-realization. You are *only* born to know the truth of life." I sat there thinking, *What on earth is he talking about?* I'd been conditioned to work hard, be successful and enjoy the fruits of success. I didn't have a clue what he meant - but I knew I was listening to truth. His words resonated deeply within me.

Breaking the Spell of Endless Desires

During my silence challenge, I realised how easily we are trapped - stuck in boring routines and activities that don't reflect our true nature to be peaceful, happy and loving. We chase external success, love and pleasure, while ignoring the silent wisdom whispering inside. Perhaps my realisations show the benefits of sitting silently for even five minutes a day.

Freedom is Found in Simplicity

When you find meaning	Freedom is there.
When you fulfil your desires	Freedom is there.
When you let go of your unfulfilled desires that do not serve you	Freedom is there.

The Three Elements

The three elements of Purpose, Freedom and Wisdom are inseparable.
> True purpose creates wisdom.
> Wisdom creates freedom.
> Freedom allows your purpose to flourish.

Meditation and Mindfulness -Truth or Fiction?

There are numerous scientific studies that prove meditation is an absolute must for brain health and optimising our decision-making. So, what's it got to do with Purpose, Freedom and Wisdom?

In 2011, a landmark study by Harvard affiliated researchers at Massachusetts Hospital, found that just eight weeks of mindfulness and meditation practice led to measurable changes in the brain.

MRI scans showed increased grey matter in areas such as the hippocampus, the cerebellum and the posterior cingulate cortex. The 'PCC' is where the mental chatter occurs - the ego's favourite playground.

These parts of the brain, house our emotional regulation, empathy, memory and self-awareness. In other words, regular meditation and conscious mindfulness give clearer introspection when these areas are rejuvenated - the brain's architecture is transformed so that we can more easily find a way to live in purpose and wisdom.

So, can you really afford to ignore the science? Ready to commit to meditation?

Your turn: Take a Selfie of Truth

You know what to do. Press *The Zen Button* first. Sit in the flow of the moment with full awareness of the *prana* in each breath.

ASK YOURSELF

Who am I when I remove the mask I wear to protect myself?

REFLECTIVE PROMPT

Analyse your thoughts. Label them -

For example, what springs to mind on the following words:

Fantasy...

Planning...

Judgement...

Regrets...

Watch the *prana* in every breath. Notice the mental chatter lose power.

Which thoughts are helping you or holding you back? You've got this! I have every faith in you.

SECRET #21

HOW TO DISCOVER YOUR PURPOSE
with a little bit of Zen

The secret wisdom whispers in your ear

To find purpose, we need to find meaning

To find meaning, we need to find our *ikigai**

To find our ikigai, we need to trust ourselves and do what we love

To find what we love, we need to trust ourselves and be honest

To be honest, we need to stop listening to others and stop fitting in with society's expectations

To be honest, we need to sacrifice our unhealthy habits and follow the path of truth

Who is truthful in this world?

Who is truthful about themselves?

Who is sincere about correcting their own mistakes?

Who is truthful and takes responsibility for their own actions?

Stand still and smell the roses

and think deeply, *what is my truth?*

Stand still and ignore the restless mind

Meditation helps bring clarity, meaning and purpose to life

Who really wants to become the local Zen master of cool?

Who really wants to discover their purpose?

MINDFUL THOUGHTS ON
FINDING PURPOSE IN LIFE

We can learn from Japanese wisdom.

Ikigai means doing what you love, doing it well, being rewarded and serving the needs of the world.

The word *oubaitouri* in Japanese philosophy represents the cherry, plum, peach and apricot trees. All flower at different times in the spring with their own unique beauty. This is a metaphor describing how we are all like flowers - blooming and growing at our own pace in our own beautiful way, without the need to compare ourselves to others.

SECRET #22

HOW TO BE WISE
without being a bighead

The secret wisdom whispers in your ear

A wise person realises they know nothing

A foolish person thinks they know everything

A wise person is humble

A foolish person is proud of their achievements

A wise person has the power to punish but chooses the higher path of forgiveness instead of punishment

A foolish person talks more than they listen

A wise person seeks more wisdom and realises their foolishness

A foolish person thinks borrowed wisdom is their own wisdom

A wise person develops wisdom from self-knowledge

Most of us oscillate between wisdom and foolishness

Most of us gain second-hand knowledge rather than first-hand wisdom

Can we attain *pure* wisdom through the experiences of others?

Can we attain *pure* wisdom by talking about the weather or what we did at the weekend?

Pure wisdom is attained through meaningful thoughts, truthful words and uplifting company

Pure wisdom is attained through our own unique life experiences

Pure wisdom is attained through detachment with love

Inner faith, inner trust, inner love and inner respect lead us to *pure* wisdom

Who really wants to be wise?

MINDFUL THOUGHTS ON BECOMING WISE

Wisdom is attained through detachment with love.
A wise person knows when to speak truthfully and when to be silent.
Approach a wise person with your questions.
If they reply, "You'll work it out," this wisdom might be the most helpful advice you ever received.

Don't Push If
The Door Says Pull

SECRET #23

HOW TO BE FREE
by stepping out of your cage

The secret wisdom whispers in your ear

We all want...
...freedom from fear
...freedom from negatives
...freedom from unhealthy habits

We all want...
...freedom from unhappiness
...from suffering
...freedom from the tiresome treadmill of daily life
...freedom from worry to express ourselves

To be FREE is our destiny
To be FREE is in our grasp
To be FREE is in our soul
To be FREE is a choice
BUT

To be FREE we need to know what freedom *really* is for each
of us...
...we need to stop trapping ourselves
...we need to start making time for ourselves

To be FREE we need to ask if we are living a life of freedom
or a life of self-imprisonment

Contemplate deeply why freedom is so difficult to attain

Contemplate why we delay what is good for us indefinitely and accept what is bad, day after day

Contemplate, *Who am I?*

To be free, we need the courage...

...to break free from our unhealthy attachments and fears

...to break free from our trapped lives

...to break free from what is unhelpful for us and create what is healthy for us

Freedom defines us...

...it is in our hands

...it is waiting for us

Freedom is what we all deserve

Freedom is absolutely possible

But HOW?

Ten practical steps to help you attain freedom...

STEP ONE

Get rid of all unnecessary desires...

...because unfulfilled desires are the root cause of our unhappiness and restrict our freedom

STEP TWO

Take responsibility for your decisions and circumstances...

...because when you take responsibility for today, you free yourself from lack of confidence and excuses of the past

STEP THREE

Create goals which are achievable...

...because when you achieve your short-term goals, you gain valuable confidence from actual results, thus giving you the inner determination to achieve your long-term goals quicker

STEP FOUR

Free yourself from all obstacles, including laziness, doubts and fears...

...because laziness, doubts and fears are tricks of the mind which trap you and hide your inner faith and superpowers

STEP FIVE

Pay off your debts...

...because debt leaves you working for the bank instead of having money in the bank working for you

STEP SIX

Waste less money...

...because spending money on what you want instead of spending money on what you need can trap you in a spiral of need and greed

STEP SEVEN

Value and appreciate what you have today...

...because postponing happiness until tomorrow, traps you indefinitely in unhappiness today

STEP EIGHT

Meditate daily. You can begin to experience freedom and loving detachment inside...

...because the REAL Freedom is inner stillness and inner happiness

STEP NINE

Try something new...

...because spontaneity and new experiences broaden your horizons and make you more interesting and interested in life

STEP TEN

Give less attention to what others think about you...

...because what matters the most is how you see and treat yourself

No more excuses.

Who really wants to be free?

MINDFUL THOUGHTS ON FREEDOM

"The secret to happiness is freedom... and the secret to freedom is courage." Thucydides, a Greek philosopher and historian.

Your state of mind defines your freedom;

Your state of health defines your freedom;

Your state of wealth defines your freedom;

Your state of consciousness defines your freedom.

Be free!

Happiness = Calmness
Unhappiness = Restlessness
What do you choose?
Both cost nothing!

CONTEMPLATION CORNER

☆ Purpose ☆ Wisdom ☆ Freedom ☆

Purpose steadies the mind.

With purpose you stay focussed on what matters and steer clear of wasting time on needless negativity.

Diverse cultures can be beautiful teachers. Reading about or being in the company of inspirational role models can boost your confidence and happiness.

HAVE YOU TAPPED INTO YOUR SISU TODAY? *Sisu* is Finnish for purpose, resilience and strength in adversity. Finland regularly wins the top spot for the happiest people in the world.

IN COSTA RICA people live a life of *pura vida* - living a life of love, freedom and joy. Love, family and friends and the connection to nature comes first. Career second.

THE NATIVE AMERICAN INDIANS have an ancient culture which flows with nature and the universe. They honour and value each individual to be as significant as the stars in the sky. I love that.

WHAT DOES FREEDOM MEAN TO YOU? WHAT STEPS CAN YOU TAKE TO MAKE YOUR LIFE FREER IN THE NEXT MONTH?

WHAT AREAS OF YOUR LIFE REPRESENT FREEDOM AND WHICH AREAS REPRESENT IMPRISONMENT?

WHO IS THE WISEST PERSON YOU KNOW? WHAT HAVE YOU LEARNT FROM THEM?

WHAT'S YOUR PURPOSE? ARE YOU LIVING IT NOW? If not, what do you need to change to add more meaning and purpose to your life?

SECRET #24

HOW TO STAY TRUE TO YOURSELF
in a world of sharks and piranhas

The secret wisdom whispers in your ear

Ethics and integrity are the pillars of truth
The pillars of a meaningful life
...of moral responsibility
...of higher values

We inherit firstly our ethics and integrity from our parents and teachers
We then develop our ethics through beliefs, knowledge and experience
When we cultivate the mind, we cultivate our own ethics and integrity

If we feed our eyes and ears with hate and extremism, slowly this *food* will become our barometer as to what's right and what's wrong
If we feed our eyes and ears with love and balance, slowly this *food* will become our barometer as to what's good and what's bad

BUT

In this world of truth and lies is a murky landscape
Ethics and morality interwoven with corruption and dishonesty...

How can we even know what is true and what is false?

By speaking *our authentic* truth and not the *borrowed* truth of others

By living *our authentic* truth and not hiding behind the truth of others

BUT, Do we know what *our own authentic* truth is anymore?

We all choose...

...how we live

...how we behave

...how we act

...how we speak

Yet be honest, my friend...

Do you take full responsibility for your own thoughts, words and deeds?

Or are you busy preaching from the back seat of the bus?

Do you admit to your faults and correct yourself?

Or are you busy telling others what faults to correct?

Contemplate deeply...

Do any of us know anymore the difference between right and wrong?

If the waiter in a restaurant forgets to charge us for drinks, do we tell them or stay silent with a smile?

Do we know how to succeed with honour and integrity?

Do we choose the narrow path of integrity or the rocky path of chicanery?

Staying true to ourselves we keep our integrity, honesty and ethics intact

...we follow our own secret wisdom

...we follow our own truth

...we lead others, by action - not words

...we admit to our mistakes and improve ourselves

Honest people live with their head held high

...sleep easy at night

...and smile silently

To live a life of integrity and achieve *meaning*, we need to eradicate our negative habits...

...we need to constantly add positive habits

To live with ethics and integrity demands conscious effort, self-reflection and discipline

Do we *really* believe we can create our destiny?

Good company makes us good

Bad company makes us bad

Sometimes the simplest words tell the simplest truth

Who really wants to live a life of truth?

MINDFUL THOUGHTS ON
STAYING TRUE TO OURSELVES

Gandhi lived by a self-imposed code of morality and ethics, centred around non-violence, self-sacrifice to serve the world, self-control, self-reliance and truth.

He advocated seven beautiful guidelines, first published in his newspaper *Young India* in 1925:

"No wealth without work.

No pleasure without conscience.

No science without humanity.

No knowledge without character.

No politics without principle.

No commerce without morality.

No worship without sacrifice."

Trust yourself. Keep good company in your head and your heart.

Keep good company amongst your friends.

"The time is always right to do what is right." Martin Luther King Jr

Remove your Mask!
The REAL fantastic YOU is hiding behind your persona

SECRET #25

HOW TO STAY CALM IN AN ARGUMENT
without saying a word

The secret wisdom whispers in your ear

To stand up for ourselves is a sign of strength

To argue for the sake of argument is a sign of weakness

Arguing only fuels anger and animosity

We argue to win instead of quietly putting across our point of view

We argue because...

...we believe we are right...

...we have strong beliefs

...and we can believe we lose face if we are silent

We argue because this world often teaches us we have to win or lose

If we argue, we lose focus on our true nature and give away our power

My friend, arguing has no value...

...to put across your view calmly is the best approach

But certainly, it's not the easiest either

If you fail, try again

If nobody listens, remain silent

If your views differ to others, so what!

If your views are forceful, you will only lose strength by trying to convert others

If your view is rejected, welcome the outcome with humility, not frustration

Do you *really* know what your own opinion is?
It's easy to be parrots and not think for ourselves
To repeat what we read
To speak badly of others

Mindful debate respects differences
To debate and learn from others is to be applauded, not dismissed...
...to be celebrated, not criticised
...to be dynamic - not to humiliate others

The secret wisdom humbly asks...
Do you practise what you preach?
Do you ask questions, but dislike the same questions being asked of you?
Do you really need others to agree with you?

What's the solution?
Be like the lotus...
...silently witnessing the drama of life...
...above the water, but rooted to the ground under the water
...detached from worldly troubles

We become masters of our destiny when we listen to *understand* rather than listen to *respond*

Who really wants to stay calm in an argument?

MINDFUL THOUGHTS ON
STAYING CALM IN AN ARGUMENT

"I am not here to be right. I am here to get it right." Brené Brown, American academic and author.

It's really not easy to be smart and walk away from an argument.

If you fail as many of us have done, be more conscious next time.

Let the fire cool down. Don't pour fuel on the fire.

Afterwards, find the moment to express yourself only if the other person is receptive.

I remember once arguing with myself. I was so annoyed; I didn't talk to myself for days!

Are you ready to stay silent and remove yourself from the next argument?

SECRET #26

HOW TO BE A GREAT LEADER
leaving your ego outside the door

The secret wisdom whispers in your ear

Great Leaders serve
Great Leaders help us to prosper
Great Leaders sacrifice their needs to humbly serve us

Great Leaders...
....educate and care
...bring prosperity to the environment
...practise what they promise
...and nurture with love and kindness

Great Leaders...
...bring peace
...bring freedom
...bring hope
...bring togetherness

My friend, where are the great leaders today?
Which leader today is *really* humble?
Which leader *trusts* us with the truth?
Which leader is *full* of compassion without an ounce of pomposity?
Which leader *devotes* their life to others with love and honesty?

Which leader has the *qualities* of leadership that *we* desire and need?

When we stop to think, do we vote for leaders who faithfully serve us and not themselves?

When we stop to think, when do we start to take responsibility for ourselves?

Who wants to be a great leader?

MINDFUL THOUGHTS ON LEADERSHIP

Be conscious. Be a great leader yourself. Be careful not to over-tech your life. Stay free.

In the not-too-distant future, world leaders might be AI-generated, monitoring our every move and dictating our lives.

Even a stroll on the beach will be monitored by our 'buddy' drone telling us...

...how far and how fast we have to walk...

...how much water we must drink...

...how often we must clean our house and change our sheets!

Social discredits or punishments may await those of us who dare to value freedom over conformity.

MINDFUL MOMENT - Be honest. In the quiet of your own conscience, ask yourself - *Am I leading my life with love and compassion or just drifting along - masking my feelings and letting events lead me, rather than taking responsibility and control of my destiny?*

Leader + Restless Mind = HUMAN

Thoughtful Leader + Calm Mind = SUPERHUMAN

CONTEMPLATION CORNER

☆ Ethics ☆ Arguments ☆ Leadership ☆

Who's your guru? Your phone? Your watch? AI?

It's not easy...

...to voice your own opinions or to follow what you believe or even know what to believe! To discover yourself more, make time each week to sit quietly for five minutes to tune into your *own* wisdom, your *own* beliefs and your *own* feelings.

Let go of the need to seek approval from others. It's a significant step worth taking. It's possible, but requires huge strength. The trick is to know who to listen to - and who to politely ignore.

When I spent 300 days in silence...

The voice I connected to in the silence was my own inner voice. My own inner feelings. My own judgements. We can only hear our true voice in silence.

YOU ALREADY KNOW WHAT HELPS YOU AND WHAT HINDERS YOU, BUT DO YOU ACTION WHAT YOU KNOW TO BE TRUE? To become great leaders, we need to be able to lead ourselves first. A chaotic personal life leads to chaotic leadership.

TIME FOR SOME MORE QUESTIONS. WHAT QUALITIES OR HABITS MIGHT HELP YOU REACH YOUR DREAMS WHILE KEEPING YOUR ETHICS AND INTEGRITY INTACT?

WHAT MATTERS TO YOU THE MOST? BE HONEST. WHAT DESIRES DO YOU HAVE LEFT TO FULFIL? Write a list and then cross out half of them that do not serve you well.

WHAT QUALITIES DO YOU HAVE TO BECOME A GREAT LEADER?

DO YOU HAVE A BUCKETLOAD OF OPINIONS ON HOW TO SOLVE THE WORLD'S PROBLEMS?

If so, think of three things you would change and HOW.

Do you feel that strongly or are you happy to remain a back seat driver?

If not, go for it and change the world.

REFLECTIONS

Great People Lead by Example

Gandhi remains one of the most humble and influential leaders in history. He fought injustice by championing nonviolence and believed when we change ourselves, others will change around us. Like all great leaders, his leadership was rooted in honesty, morality and unwavering integrity. He lived a disciplined life leading by example.

If we don't 'lead' ourselves to change our habits and patterns, we are unlikely to achieve the *happy, meaningful success* we desire.

Is Ambition Healthy?

Excessive ambition propels us down an uncertain path, hurtling us towards a vision of success that may never happen. It's possible to be successful and driven by fear - but success built on fear won't make us happy, free or wise. Many financially successful people live in fear of losing their wealth - so much so that they barely spend money and continue to overwork, driven by anxiety rather than learning to *Just Be*.

We need to decide if our ambition is driven by unlimited greed and never-ending desires or an ambition that benefits others as well as ourselves.

The Dreaded 'D' Word

It's time to discuss the dreaded 'D' word. *Discipline.*

There's no way of getting around it.

No discipline = No success. Meaningful or otherwise.

Let's say you are learning a language. If you commit to learn fifteen words each day but skip here and there, you will not only lose retention of the words you learnt, but will end up losing an extra fifteen words a day. Miss too many days and you will create a negative momentum leading to quitting.

Failure doesn't appear overnight.

Failure and frustration happen because of the momentum we create.

In the same way, if you commit to sending ten emails each day to new clients, if you do fifteen instead, you are five ahead already. The good and bad fruits are the result of our actions or inaction. If you want to accomplish your goals, you will need discipline.

Discipline takes control of time. Without discipline, time takes control of you.

How to Give Up a Bad Habit

Changing ourselves means reprogramming and disciplining our minds and bodies to be healthy, because it's good for us! What we consume deeply affects the way we think, feel and behave.

In India, there was a revered spiritual teacher called Ramakrishna Paramahamsa. People travelled from afar to seek his wisdom.

One day, a woman brought along her young son. Her son refused to eat food, only sweets. She asked the master to tell her son to stop eating sweets. The master looked at her and remained silent. Week after week, she returned with the same request. Still, Ramakrishna remained silent. Finally, on the fourth week, he told the boy gently, "Eat healthy food. Sweets are ok sometimes - but not all the time." The mother was relieved but also confused. "Why didn't you say this earlier?" she asked. He replied, "Because I eat sweets every day. I had to stop first, otherwise I couldn't give your son advice in good conscience."

It's easy to give advice when we haven't quit our own unhelpful habits. Real influence starts with personal change.

A Puff of Smoke

When I was eleven, I puffed on my first cigarette with my older sister. We thought we looked cool, like movie stars, but minutes later our faces turned white and we felt sick.

Fast Forward 10 years

It was my first day as a Eurobond trader, one of the most stressful jobs imaginable. By then, I was smoking a packet a day. Despite my early negative experience of smoking and the occasional chest pain, it hadn't deterred my lack of mind control to harm my body. That evening, as a show of mental strength (to myself), I made the decision, *I'm quitting smoking.* Just like that. The habit was kicked.

How could I do it? Quite simply because *I* made a clear, firm decision. I told my mind - *we* are quitting.

Fast Forward Another 10 years

I had just started meditating. My career was flying and so was my stress. On my 31st birthday I went out for dinner and ate a fillet steak. The next morning, I woke up and decided - *no more eating animals.* Just like that! Again, no willpower, no debate. It happened. A shift from inside. The desire just left me.

I went from carnivore to vegetarian to vegan. Shortly after, I gave up alcohol. It was a natural event without any thought. Again, the desire left me. 'Drinking' friends left me too!

Fear: The Most Effective Way to Quit a Bad Habit!

My friend Jonathan, smoked three packets of cigarettes per day for 40 years. At 60, he had a heart attack. After surgery, his first words to the Doctor were "Is it ok if I have a cigarette now?" The doctor smiled. "Sure - if you want another heart attack." Jonathan never touched a cigarette again.

Fear is a powerful motivator. Make positive changes instead of waiting for a health issue to make the changes for you.

The Power of the Mind

We've just explored three real examples of how to quit unhealthy habits by using the power *behind* the mind.

1) Quitting through willpower and conscious decision making - giving the mind no choice.
2) Quitting naturally without effort.
3) Quitting because of fear.

There's a fourth category too, which applies to many of us - struggling to quit a bad habit we find hard to break even though we try to do so. Quitting gradually.

To Change Ourselves, We Need to Be Honest

When we're honest with ourselves, we make time to do whatever we want. We make and break our own rituals and rules. Some of us *can't* start the day without coffee. Others *need* the gym. Some *must* have a cigarette. We create a mixed bag of rituals.

THE BIG SECRET? You know it already - to create rituals which are healthy for us.

When we *really* want something, we do it, even if the mind or body objects. But when we don't feel we have to, we procrastinate daily, even if the outcome benefits us.

We waste our most valuable asset every day - TIME.

So, the big question is - do we use time on what supports and strengthens us - or drift along and build up what is unhelpful for our growth?

Quitting Gradually Works

To quit a bad habit requires positive motivation and it's often easier to do in small steps.

If you smoke fifteen cigarettes per day, reduce to fourteen per day this week. Thirteen next week, and so on. In four months' time you'll be at zero. When the craving comes, eat something healthy instead. Direct replacement helps the mind form new habits.

My Story with Sugar

When I was eight, I was shipped off to boarding school. My best friend added sugar to his cornflakes. I copied him. Two sugars in his tea. I followed.

Years later, after quitting smoking, I decided to cut back on sugar too. I did it gradually...

☆ Day 1   from 2 sugars   →   1.5 sugars
☆ 1 month later   from 1.5 sugars in my tea   →   1 sugar
☆ 2 months later from 1 sugar   →   ½ sugar
☆ 3 months later *Sugar Free Tea*

When change is gradual it doesn't feel like loss.

Reward Yourself

Every time you cut down or quit a habit, set aside the money you're saving. Celebrate your success. Give yourself a big treat:

A dream holiday; a deposit for a car or maybe a gift for someone you love.

If your mind strays, focus on the health benefits, your big treat and the goal ahead.

Still not convinced? Calculate how much money your bad habit has cost you over the last ten years. Write down the number in big bold letters. What else could you have done with the money?

Summary: How To Break a Bad Habit

Consider implementing the following:

1) Decide 100% you want to change.
2) Write down the clear benefits of quitting.
3) Focus your attitude on the goal.
4) Take it slowly.
5) If you slip up, continue.
6) Make small, incremental changes
7) When temptation comes, replace the habit with a healthy treat.
8) Keep an emergency supply of healthy snacks to hand.
9) Track your new savings, and reward yourself.

Remember, the same mind that traps you can also set you free. If you can quit any bad habit, it's proof that you can overcome any challenge ahead.

Go For It!

LIFE IS CHAOTIC

Unhappy Chaos = Doubt and Fear

Happy Chaos   = Confidence and Love

No Chaos   = Success, Contentment & Peace

MOTIVATION ZONE

Doubts, confusion and questions will continue until you stop and listen to what you really want. This begins with a commitment from yourself - to question the beliefs that limit you and to break down the barriers that keep you from living the life you want and deserve. To reject what's not working and to fully immerse in what's good for you. You can then redefine success on your own terms - to cultivate a life of meaning and clarity.

Giving Away Your Power

To keep our focus on purpose, wisdom and freedom, we need a constant flow of positive energy and to learn how to retain this power.

One of the biggest realisations in my silence challenge, was how easily we give away our power - at work, in our relationships and even how we react to news.

Lesson 1: Mind Your Own Business

On my daily walk, I was struck by how silence increased my awareness. I was appalled to witness my mind judging strangers; constantly. How they dressed, how they walked and even why a clothes shop might fail, applying my business mind!

"MYOB, David", I kept telling myself.

This was a shocking realisation of my mind wasting time and energy on total strangers. Who am I to judge what people wear? This bad habit also carries over to when our inner critic silently judges friends and family.

Lesson 2: Calmly Act. Don't Overreact.

One day in silence I watched a woman walking with a colleague going down a path to the river. Her attention was distracted. She walked straight into a traffic bollard in the middle of the path. It must have hurt like hell. She winced, brushed herself off and carried on walking and talking as if nothing had happened.

I was amazed. I knew if it were me in her position I would have cursed and stopped. But she collected her composure and carried on.

This taught me another valuable lesson.

Too often, we give away our power, overreact or allow events to dictate our lives. The woman remained calm and non-reactive. I thought, *This is how to learn from being the silent witness.*

Ask Yourself

"How many times today did I give away my power?"

- ✧ To anger
- ✧ To pride
- ✧ To ego
- ✧ To fear
- ✧ To negative memories
- ✧ To negative thoughts
- ✧ To negative emotions
- ✧ To events I cannot control
- ✧ To unnecessary desires
- ✧ To pain and suffering
- ✧ To wasting time
- ✧ To foolishness
- ✧ To unhappiness

Each of these apply to our inner world - our thoughts, emotions and actions - but also how we respond to others.

If you can recognise these inner patterns, then in my view, you've already taken the big step towards real personal growth. When I look at the list I also slip up time and time again! But, I don't give up and nor should you.

Flip the Switch - Taking Back Control

1) Take your time to note down how giving away your power has impacted your life. Be honest. Keep your answers close to hand for easy reference. Reflect deeply.
2) If you feel anger or regret, allow it. Be the witness. When you are ready, let it go.
3) Are you ready to change?
4) Start with kindness and non-judgement. None of us can change yesterday. Only today.
5) Choose your top three. The ones that drain your power the most. Track them daily. See how and why they show up. Change begins by paying attention.

Reclaiming Your Power Step by Step

Keep focussing on the *prana* within each breath. Breathing in positive energy and exhaling negativity.

Start to notice what shifts. When you change the inner narrative, what changes? Start to experience the path to:

✧ Calmness
✧ Humility
✧ Selflessness
✧ Love
✧ Positive memories

✧ Positive thoughts
✧ Positive emotions
✧ To what you can control
✧ To meaningful desires
✧ To wellbeing and contentment
✧ To making the most of time
✧ To being smart
✧ To happiness

Remember, transformation doesn't happen overnight, but nothing changes if we remain stuck in the mud. Everything starts when you make the conscious decision to change.

I have a feeling you just made the decision. You can do it!

Freedom Framework

How about creating a *Freedom Framework* to dismantle any mental or emotional barriers that hold you back time and time again?

✧ You feel	Uncertain about your life's direction. Held back by fear of the unknown.
✧ You tell yourself	*I'm afraid of making the wrong choices. I don't know what to do. I'm trapped and unsure of my purpose.*
✧ Flip the Switch	*Fear is just a sign that I'm stepping into something new. So What! I have the power to create my own freedom. I will persevere. By exploring what truly matters to me, I am uncovering my path. I trust that with each choice I make, I am stepping closer to clarity and a life of meaning. I am open to seeing difficulties as an opportunity for growth.*

TAKE ACTION

What does your *Freedom Framework* look like?

Complete the three sentences:

1. I feel free when I ....
2. I feel most trapped when I ....
3. I want to live a life where I ....

Now circle the word which feels the most important to you from your answers. Make that your *power* word for the week - to remind you of who you're becoming.

What's Your Purpose?

✧ YOU FEEL	Confused about Your purpose.
✧ YOU TELL YOURSELF	*My purpose is unclear. I'm torn between following my passion and earning a living.*
✧ FLIP THE SWITCH	*I am worthy of a meaningful life. My purpose is unfolding. I am ready to define my life. Every day, I will use my power to bridge the gap between my thoughts and my accomplishments. I will focus on my values and passions, trusting that the right signal will guide me in time.*

TAKE ACTION

ASK YOURSELF

What is my message to the world? Reflect on your values and passions. You are now looking at yourself without criticism. Be inspired! You have so much to offer.

Do You Feel Judged?

We want to be loved and accepted without judgement. But do we love others in the same way? We have touched on the negative effect of self-criticism so how can we overcome others judging us and hurting us through criticism? Only by being detached with love.

If Nobody Judged Me, I Would...

What's your first thought to complete the sentence? About work? What you wear? Where you live? When to say no? Do you have a dream buried deep inside, hidden by your fears of being judged by others?

Be bold. When you let go of the fear of being judged, you gain back your control and power.

Mini Reflections

List three activities that give you energy

1.

2.

3.

List three activities that give you meaning

1.

2.

3.

Wisdom Cultivation

Wisdom is a state of being where you can sit comfortably without knowing all of the answers. My greatest successes come from following my inner guidance and wisdom rather than popular opinions of the crowd.

Perception is the starting point to wisdom.

Embrace uncertainty and *be compassionately detached*.

Mini Reflection

Keep a note of what is stored in the back of your mind which is of positive value - not as final answers but as living questions.

Which Mistake in Your Life Has Taught You The Most?

Full freedom and self-realisation don't arrive all at once. Enjoy the glimpses of freedom in every conscious breath. *Trust Yourself! You know the way.*

PART FIVE

SUCCESS
AMBITION & CAREER

Create a Career that Counts

SUCCESS AMBITION & CAREER

In Part Five, we start with a commentary about seizing our opportunities, along with reflections from my 300 days in silence. Then back to the quiet whispering wisdom; bite-sized secrets about success, entrepreneurship, your career and finally, humility. All hopefully with a touch of humour that keeps the serious stuff light. Then back to Contemplation Corner, reflections on money and Motivation Zone to inspire positivity when you're having an off day.

> *"Opportunity should not be*
> *neglected for it may never return."*
> Baba Hariharananda, revered yogi from India.

Golden Opportunity

Once upon a time, the God of Money and the God of Compassion were discussing a man who always complained he never received any help. The God of Money explained he always tried to help, but the man never accepted the opportunities given to him. The God of Compassion suggested they give him one more chance.

To ensure their plan was completely foolproof, they placed a large lump of gold just ten metres ahead of where the man was walking. It was impossible to miss - the gold would change his life, forever.

As the man approached, he noticed a blind man walking next to him. Instead of offering a helping hand, he closed his eyes to imagine what it was like to be blind. He stepped over the lump of gold and kept walking.

I love this story. It teaches us that help and support is always around us, often in unexpected ways. If we walk with our heads held high and eyes open, we see life's opportunities. We celebrate and appreciate life. If we walk around with our heads down and eyes closed, we miss life and all the possibilities.

It's Your Choice

The last story is a beautiful metaphor about every aspect of life, especially our ambitions. Opportunities are everywhere, but pass us by if we aren't paying attention.

Humility is the tiny seed that gives the opportunity for growth. Effort is the soil, the water is the fertiliser - the foundation to success. Growth is steady and sustainable when built on solid ground. Success requires tenacity, smart decision making and focussed effort. Since childhood, I've always wanted to learn *HOW*. If I didn't know *HOW*, I asked. If I didn't understand, I asked until I understood fully. Pride and ego are forms of self-sabotage when it comes to success. I am reminded of the old motto, "Don't ask, don't get!"

The Silence Revelation: Success Beyond Convention

During my silence, I thought deeply about every aspect of life - love, faith, family, relationships, success and purpose. All the topics covered in *The Big Secret of How*. I wondered, would my football team perform better if they learnt the secrets of breath control?

Is it right to use spiritual practices to gain material success?

Why did my auditors appear in my dreams brandishing machine guns?

Here are a few more reflections from my silence diary.

* * * SILENCE DIARY EXTRACTS * * *

Day 2: What's of Value?

"I'm reading about a lama from Tibet. He confirms what Baba told me - *"The time spent doing spiritual practice is the only time spent which will have lasting value."* I think deeply about this advice. It goes against the grain of what I was taught - to chase my dreams of financial success regardless of the emotional, physical and mental consequences. We buy things we don't need or can't afford - living with the frustration of unaccomplished goals. Life becomes a pressure cooker and it's our hands turning up the heat."

[No wonder it is estimated that in the UK one in four suffer from mental health issues and one in seven take anti-depressants.]

* * *

Day 20: Success is in The Breath

"Football has been a big part of my life. In fact, it's the first time since I was a young kid that I've not known the results.

I reflect how much better my team Arsenal would perform if they knew about the hidden yogic principles about breath to reduce injuries as well as boosting performance. Success and failure are in the finest of details. The smallest advantage makes all the difference. A yogi knows how to tip the odds through mastery of the *prana*; yet I wonder if using spiritual powers is ethical for gain in the world."

* * *

Day 108: Whose Success is it Anyway?

"12.08-1.31pm, meditate. Mind still.
Contemplate achievement and pride.

How can I claim success if I am only the *instrument* - fully reliant on the help of others? There seems to be a universal order and timing to everything. Like it or not, we can't control it. I tried for years to sell my business; it just wouldn't happen. Then one day, it happened effortlessly. I was never driven by recognition. Achievements soon become history. Who cares? It's why we are born with our eyes in the front of the head and not at the back. I perceive and believe more and more that *all* is being done through us. That feels strangely kind of comforting."

* * *

By the end of my silence, I had completely redefined what success means to me. Having built a business and achieving the conventional markers of success, I realised...

Success has little to do with external validation and everything to do with internal alignment. Success isn't defined by achievements alone, but importantly who you *become* in the process. When your purpose, values and actions are in sync, that's when *real being* and fulfilment begin. And there's nothing wrong with enjoying the fruits of your effort and discipline - you deserve it.

My Story - Success Has Many Parents - Failure Has None

Before Part One, I wrote four words... *Be Great, Be Grateful.*

If you forget everything else, please remember these four words. These words will lift you when times are tough and ground you when success goes to your head.

When I left my business after it was sold, my final day was emotional. I was saying goodbye to the baby I had nurtured with love for almost 20 years. Some team members had been with me from the beginning. In my farewell speech I thanked the thousands of people (not there that day) who had supported us - Tony the printer, Pete the stationery guy, John the corporate gift guy, the clients, everyone...

Without help we cannot achieve anything. Gratitude gives success meaning.

Your Turn - When Did You Last Take a Look at Your Personal Balance Sheet?

In finance, I learnt how to analyse a company's balance sheet to understand its true financial position. You now know we can do this for ourselves by regularly doing a self-audit with the *Selfie of Truth*. It can be applied to everything. A balance sheet is a snapshot of today - the result of *every* yesterday in your life.

For instance, you can do a *health* balance sheet - if you've lifted heavy boxes or bags for years without taking care of your posture, then your back will become a liability affecting the rest of your life as a fast-depreciating asset!

What health aspect is affecting *you* due to lack of self-awareness? If you've identified the issue are you carrying on or ready to change? Taking pills or visiting doctors isn't enough. We have to take responsibility and manage our own health.

Self-analysis of our balance sheet today, helps us know what to change and build a better tomorrow. At the end of Part Six we'll do a complete life balance sheet. For now, a quick financial check -

☆ What's your bank balance?   ☆ What are your savings?   ☆

☆ What are your assets?   ☆ What are your liabilities? ☆

☆ How much is coming in and how much is going out each month?

☆ How do you feel when you review your financial health? Good? Bad? Sad?

☆ Don't worry. When you change your mindset, you can change your finances. What's your financial goal for the next 12 months? In three years? In five years?

Surely you will make it possible if you want it enough.

SECRET #27

HOW TO BE A GREAT SUCCESS
by being street smart

The secret wisdom whispers in your ear

The university of life is *the* university that counts the most

It rewards our efforts and encourages us to overcome our weaknesses

The university of life is unavoidable

Like it or not...

...life teaches us that our actions and choices create...

...success and failure

...joy and suffering

Obtaining a degree shows we have developed our abilities to master a topic

AND

Our academic achievements give us the opportunity to stand out in the crowded field

AND

The best chance to secure the top jobs

BUT

Our academic achievements of yesterday won't pay the bills of today

Once our career begins, academic success becomes yesterday's news

Our successes will manifest through...

...common sense...ability...attitude...skills...honesty...results

Success and failure are both in our hands

If we want success, we must learn from our failures

If we really want success enough, we will get it

Go-getters constantly hone the mind to achieve, improve and succeed

They achieve small successes daily and live life with unswerving authenticity

Go-getters overcome adversity with laser-like focus,

turning their dreams into reality

Go-getters master life, the mind and destiny itself!

They commit to their own unique path, regardless of the opinion of others

Go-getters who are full of consciousness humbly treat others with love, respect and kindness

Who wants to be a Great Success?

MINDFUL THOUGHTS
ON BEING A GREAT SUCCESS

"Often we look so long at the closed door, we do not see the one that has been opened for us." Helen Keller, author and disability rights champion.

Go-getters spend every waking moment on what's important to reach their goal.

Go-getters create time to develop themselves consciously.

If you did gain a degree with blood, sweat and tears, *really* well done. How can you use your hard-earned degree to your advantage?

If you didn't study for a degree (like me), that's ok! Educate and study yourself.

"Know then thyself, presume not God to scan; The proper study of mankind is man." Alexander Pope, 18th century British poet.

Your biggest failure is to neglect to take the opportunities in front of you.
Your second biggest failure is to focus on your weaknesses instead of maximising your strengths, talents and skills.
Why accept failure when success is calling you?

SECRET #28

HOW TO FIND MEANINGFUL SUCCESS
before you burn out

The secret wisdom whispers in your ear

Success is whatever you want it to be

One person's failure is another person's success

But will your idea of success bring happiness and contentment?

What is Meaningful Success?

Success becomes meaningful when

it's anchored in truth

it builds gradually

it creates space for others

and it becomes greater than us

Talking about success won't make you successful

My friend, is it not true that...

Successful people realise that *meaningful* success is true success?

Successful people cultivate big successes by accumulating small successes?

Consider these wise words...

Never make the same mistake twice

Learn from the mistakes of others

Don't be greedy and always leave something for the next person

Focus on the goal and not the sacrifice and suffering

Successful people relieve the suffering of others......are humble...have faith

Successful people realise their achievements are due to the help of others,

find a solution to every problem, and achieve far more than their dreams

The Prize of Success is Contentment

The Prize of Life is Contentment

The Prize of Faith is Contentment

Meditation helps you to be successful because the best ideas arrive when the mind is still

Who really wants to find meaningful success?

MINDFUL THOUGHTS ON MEANINGFUL SUCCESS

"Wealth consists not in having great possessions, but in having few wants." Epictetus, the Greek philosopher from the 1st century.

Be inspired by even your smallest successes, think about what you really want and...

Get On With It!

MEANINGFUL PROMPT - List three things that make your life meaningful

1.

2.

3.

"Success is not the key to happiness. Happiness is the key to success. If you love what you are doing, you will be successful."

Albert Schweitzer,
Nobel Peace prize winner and philosopher.

SECRET #29

HOW TO BECOME AN ENTREPRENEUR
building a business with purpose

The secret wisdom whispers in your ear

Sit silently, my friend, and listen carefully

The word entrepreneur dates back to 13th century France

Entre means 'between' & *Prendre* means 'to take'...

The entrepreneur finds the opportunity to optimise the smallest gap in the crowded market

The entrepreneur converts theory into practice...

...grabs the opportunity that others cannot see

...remodels what others have done, but does it better

The true entrepreneur maximises the potential in front of them...

...constantly improves their business and themselves

...loves what they do

The smart entrepreneur minimises the risks...

...stacks the cards in their favour

...never gambles without weighing up the odds

To be a successful entrepreneur, we need to convert theory into practice...

...we need to realise that our need to sell is greater than our client's need to buy

...we need to leave the beach and start swimming

High achievers find time to meditate every day to create a mind with clarity, focus and purpose

Who wants to become an entrepreneur?

MINDFUL THOUGHTS ON BECOMING AN ENTREPRENEUR

Have the courage to be a perfectionist who isn't perfect.

If you never start, you will never finish. Business success is about asking the right questions - not having all the answers.

Choose your advisers carefully... It's better to ask advice from one person who knows what they are talking about, than from one hundred people who don't have a clue!

REFLECTION

What's one business lesson you have learnt which has stuck with you?

SUCCESSFUL ENTREPRENEURS FOLLOW THREE MOTTOS

GID: Get It Done!

ABT: Always Be Thinking (with purpose)

KISS: Keep It Simple, Stupid

Success comes when we serve our clients with care and sincerity.

Every invoice from my company included the words:

"We are pleased to have been of service."

SECRET #30

HOW TO MAKE A PROFIT
before you go broke

The secret wisdom whispers in your ear

Making a profit is the purpose of business
Sounds obvious, but...
...the majority of businesses are just surviving on a wing and a prayer
Making a profit is neither easy nor difficult...
Sounds obvious, but making a loss is extremely easy and common!

If money isn't your thing, feel free to make more to give more to others
A few words of warning, my friend...
Surprises come daily
Not always pleasant surprises
Leave half your excess profits in the bank
to use for surprises or opportunities

If we aim high in all that we do, we go high
If we aim low or wander aimlessly, we will end up in trouble

To make a profit, we need to understand three basic business principles:
One sizzling summer doesn't mean four sweltering summers will follow
One clever idea doesn't mean success is certain

One spark of brilliance only transforms into reality through hard work and tenacity

Innovative products don't sell themselves

Promising products are rarely as great as we think

Breakthrough products that impress your friends and family are not proof of success

To run a sustainable business, cutting margins isn't the way

To run a sustainable business, we need to realise that risk doesn't always mean reward

To run a sustainable business is the journey of the few

It's the bottom line after tax that counts

It's the bottom line that tells the truth

We can't eat yields

We can't eat margins unless the volume is there

We can't eat well if a business is built on sand

At the beginning we have to compromise...

...we have to deal with clients we may not work with again

...we have to earn less and spend less

At the beginning and all the way to the end, we will never stop learning or finessing our business

To make a sustainable profit, we need to become very smart

Getting paid is number one

Getting smart means being paid before we pay our suppliers

Getting smart means we keep minimal or zero stock...

...we document every deal

...we're straight with our dealings

...we deliver what we have promised

Getting smart means keeping our overheads low and our ethics high

Always under-promise and over-deliver

Never over-promise and under-deliver

Always maximise profits on best-selling products

Never chase opportunities which glisten with fool's gold

Always give a service with a genuine smile

The inconvenient often brutal truth is...

Nobody really cares about our problems in business

Nobody really cares in business about our pain and suffering

Nobody is waiting for us

Who really wants to make a profit?

MINDFUL THOUGHTS ON MAKING A PROFIT

Profit creation works hand in hand with value creation.

The clearer you are about the value of what you offer, the more natural the path to profit becomes.

Smart people like you never give up.

Smart people like you think positively over and over again.

An accumulation of small profits leads to big profits.

Ignoring small mistakes leads to big mistakes later. Proceed with confidence not arrogance.

Purpose without profit becomes empty; purpose without profit is unsustainable.

ACTION HINT

How about setting aside 1% of next month's profits for charity?

TRY THE 15 BREATHS FOR SUCCESS

Pause for a moment. *Happy, meaningful success* is surely coming to you.

Sit outside in the fresh air. Spine straight. Inhale and exhale through the nostrils slowly. Deep, calm breathing.

Gentle attention in the centre of the forehead. Be conscious of the life-force.

1. Inhale and exhale three times thinking POSITIVITY with every inhalation.
2. Inhale and exhale three times thinking COURAGE with every inhalation
3. Inhale and exhale three times thinking PURITY with every inhalation.
4. Inhale and exhale three times thinking LOVE with every inhalation.
5. Inhale and exhale three times thinking SUCCESS with every inhalation.

Send the words through your very being!

SECRET #31

HOW TO SELL YOUR BUSINESS
at the right moment

The secret wisdom whispers in your ear

Selling a business is a rollercoaster of emotions
Selling a business needs a strategy
Selling a business needs preparation

Firstly, be honest, my friend

Does your business have real value?
Does your business have loyal clients who return year after year?
Does your business increase profits every year?
Does your business have proof of continued success?

Buyers buy potential and existing profits
Buyers want value for money
Buyers expect a high return on their capital

To build a business takes time, patience and dynamism
To build a business means fighting for every deal and client
To build a business needs confidence, skill and tenacity

To sell a business we need to reach a critical turnover
...we need to have a pipeline of brilliant products
To sell a business we need to prove it has strong foundations

Who really wants to sell their business?

MINDFUL THOUGHTS
ON SELLING YOUR BUSINESS

From my own direct experience...

Avoid being sucked in to 'professional' valuations.

The value of your business is worth only what someone is willing to pay, not what you or your advisers think it's worth.

Plan ahead. Create a seller's pack well before due diligence.

Choose a very smart and humble commercial lawyer to represent you.

An arrogant lawyer on either side of the table will destroy the deal.

Where possible, agree a fixed fee.

Advisers can and *will* make or break a deal.

Trust yourself. Remove any clauses or terms you don't understand or think are unfair.

SECRET #31

HOW TO SELL YOUR BUSINESS
at the right moment

The secret wisdom whispers in your ear

Selling a business is a rollercoaster of emotions
Selling a business needs a strategy
Selling a business needs preparation

Firstly, be honest, my friend

Does your business have real value?
Does your business have loyal clients who return year after year?
Does your business increase profits every year?
Does your business have proof of continued success?

Buyers buy potential and existing profits
Buyers want value for money
Buyers expect a high return on their capital

To build a business takes time, patience and dynamism
To build a business means fighting for every deal and client
To build a business needs confidence, skill and tenacity

To sell a business we need to reach a critical turnover
...we need to have a pipeline of brilliant products
To sell a business we need to prove it has strong foundations

Who really wants to sell their business?

MINDFUL THOUGHTS
ON SELLING YOUR BUSINESS

From my own direct experience...

Avoid being sucked in to 'professional' valuations.

The value of your business is worth only what someone is willing to pay, not what you or your advisers think it's worth.

Plan ahead. Create a seller's pack well before due diligence.

Choose a very smart and humble commercial lawyer to represent you.

An arrogant lawyer on either side of the table will destroy the deal.

Where possible, agree a fixed fee.

Advisers can and *will* make or break a deal.

Trust yourself. Remove any clauses or terms you don't understand or think are unfair.

CONTEMPLATION CORNER

☆ Success ☆ Meaningful Success ☆
☆ Entrepreneurship ☆ Making a Profit ☆
☆ Selling a Business ☆

Now's the big moment to move from perspiration to inspiration. Let go of fear. Choose courage. Radiate positivity.

The lightbulb moment is coming

Success is about doing our best in every situation, whether cooking dinner, taking care of a friend in need, motivating others, advancing in our careers through merit, or making a stranger smile.

You don't need to master everything to be successful. And, if we are honest, sometimes none of us can be bothered and our attitude stinks!

Life is super challenging

We have to overcome constant challenges in our daily lives. To change, or even recognise that behaviours and patterns which are detrimental to our progress need discarding, can be like climbing a huge mountain without ever knowing how close we are to the top. Instead of moving onwards and upwards, we can often feel we are walking backwards downhill! With the right mindset, the mountain becomes a molehill to walk around or step over.

When we shift our attitude, we change our mind. Where there's a will, there are a dozen ways. Stay positive. Don't give up! If you fail, try again.

WHAT ARE YOU PREPARED TO DO TO TRANSFORM YOUR IDEAS OF SUCCESS INTO REALITY, WITHOUT THE FEAR OF FAILURE?

IF YOU RUN A BUSINESS OR WORK FOR A COMPANY, CALCULATE YOUR HOURLY RATE. WRITE IT DOWN HERE…Happy with your take-home pay or not?

HOW CAN YOU INCREASE YOUR REWARD SO YOUR EFFORTS BECOME MORE WORTHWHILE? If money isn't your main motivation, then donate more to causes that matter to you - but never undervalue or undersell yourself.

WHICH BUSINESS IDEA OR CAREER CHANGE DO YOU WANT TO MAKE A REALITY?

SECRET #32

HOW TO NEGOTIATE YOUR SALARY
like a pro

The secret wisdom whispers in your ear

Does life give us what we deserve or what we think we
deserve?
Do we think we deserve more?

Does life offer us opportunity, or is life unfair?
Do we help or hinder ourselves?
Do we feel sorry for ourselves?

Does life help us to be our best friend or our worst enemy?
Do we love ourselves or harm ourselves?

If we deserve more, we will get more
If we deserve a pay rise, we will get a pay rise

The secret is knowing how to ask...
...how to justify our contribution
...how to justify our value
The secret is to be outstanding in all that we do and to pick
the best moment to ask

The back of the envelope tells the truth
To start the process...
Scribble down your salary and benefits...

Scribble down key moments which show how brilliant and irreplaceable you are

Write down what you want to achieve and earn, now and in the future

Avoid the trap of comparing yourself, your skillset and worth, to colleagues when justifying a pay-rise

Make a compelling presentation on...
✧ your achievements and efforts
✧ your intrinsic and financial value to the company
✧ why your boss should give you the pay rise you want
✧ your overall benefits to the company

There's an old rule which says
Employers aim to earn three times your salary
Great employers reward those who are outstanding
Great employers breed successful people

Give your boss no choice but to say yes

Who wants to negotiate their salary like a pro?

❀

MINDFUL THOUGHTS ON NEGOTIATING YOUR SALARY LIKE A PRO

Loyalty should not be confused with naivety or being taken for granted.
Value yourself and value your skills.

Loyalty is worth last month's salary and stretches no further than your performance next quarter.

Be confident. Be straight. Be popular! Yes popular. Likeable people get promoted.

If your employer doesn't value you, then find one that does!

SECRET #33

HOW TO THINK LIKE A SPIRITUAL BILLIONAIRE
without selling your soul for success

The secret wisdom whispers in your ear

Why bother aspiring to be a billionaire?
Do you believe that wealth brings happiness?
Needy people become greedy people
Greedy people become miserable people
Miserable people spread misery to others

If we always need more, we appreciate what we have less
If we keep chasing for more, we get stress and extra stress
If we always want more, we become greedy for more

Rich people think about money all day long
Poor people think about money all day long ...understandably so
Rich people often pursue happiness from never-ending wealth and power

THE BIG SECRET is to be a Spiritual Billionaire

Unlimited inner health...inner wealth...inner peace...inner joy
When we meditate daily, our spiritual billionaire journey begins......
The fruits of our joy and laughter will enrich those around us

The fruits of our positive actions and humility will spread joy to the many

Yogis believe that the fruits of our meditation continue when we leave this world

Who really wants to be a *Spiritual Billionaire*?

MINDFUL THOUGHTS ON THINKING
LIKE A SPIRITUAL BILLIONAIRE

If you really want to be a moneybags billionaire, marry one, preferably 70 years older than you with no kids.

If you really want to become a spiritual billionaire, then ditch the ego and meditate.

Spiritual billionaires help a billion people.

REFLECTION: What does *enough* look like for you?

SECRET #34

HOW TO MASTER THE ART OF HUMILITY
after success has come

The secret wisdom whispers in your ear

One small success won't...
...change your life...rocket you to your final destination...
...make or break you...pay tomorrow's bills

"All the world's a stage and all the men and women merely players"
So, if this life's a play, let's play...

Let's assume you've achieved greatness
...you've achieved financial success...
...you've achieved all that you need
...you no longer need to work for money

As you stand in the cold and rain, waiting for the bus, close your eyes and imagine...
Success has arrived
The bus is no longer needed as the chauffeur now awaits your call
Now what?

Now comes the void......the big moment...the silence
No more the need to work or the need to save

No longer any need to dress to the nines to convince ourselves or anyone else that we matter

No longer the need to appear wealthier than our reality

You can now afford to eat whatever you want

But can you eat ten meals at once?

You can now afford the finest wines

But can you keep the finest wine in the body for more than a few hours?

You can now afford the finest clothes and shoes

But can your body wear more than one pair of shoes or more than one jacket?

You can now afford the best healthcare

But will your lifestyle help you avoid needing the best healthcare?

It's easy to chase and chase, my friend, until it's too late...
Remember:

A dying person with millions will give it all up for one more breath

A dying person, rich or poor, takes nothing with them

A dying person will remember their regrets

Both the dying millionaire and the humble servant leave the world the same way

Humble people are fortunate people...staying balanced with or without money

Humble people appreciate what life has delivered and not what life has failed to deliver

Humble people find contentment regardless of circumstances

Who wants to master the art of humility?

MINDFUL THOUGHTS ON HUMILITY

We all arrive in the world with *nada* and we all leave the world with *nada*.

Your new shining Ferrari will be left behind with my 20-year-old scratched Toyota.

Instead of buying expensive designer clothes for a year, how about giving the same amount of money to charity?

"Humility is not thinking less of yourself, it's thinking of yourself less." C.S. Lewis

ACTION: Do something kind for someone today without telling anyone.

Success = *Contentment*
Contentment = *Happiness*

CONTEMPLATION CORNER

☆ Success ☆ Humility ☆ Money ☆

Which do you choose? Can you have all three?

Still yawning? When you finish this book, you'll be a changed person, ready to realise your dreams. Decide here and now to be *superhuman* and really put into practice dynamic changes before you become old and grey. Already a few grey hairs? No matter. It's never too late.

WHAT DOES SUCCESS MEAN TO YOU? Write down what comes into your head.

DO YOU FEEL VALUED AT YOUR JOB? ARE YOU OVER-WORKED AND UNDERPAID? IS YOUR CAREER MAKING YOU HAPPY?

HOW MUCH MONEY DO YOU WASTE EACH MONTH? HOW MUCH ARE YOU READY TO SAVE TO MAKE ONE OF YOUR DREAMS COME TRUE?

WHAT DOES HUMILITY MEAN TO YOU?

REFLECTIONS

Trading Places

After Big Bang, the deregulation of the financial markets in 1987, suddenly everyone and their mother was buying shares. I dabbled for a few years, playing the markets - sometimes winning, sometimes losing. In the end, I quit. Why? Because watching the value of investments go up and down was stressful and time-consuming. I decided the best way to invest my hard-earned money and time was in myself.

Today, trading has become easier than checking out at a supermarket. Just because it's easy doesn't mean it's smart. Trading must never become an emotional journey. Hunches, overconfidence or greed can't replace insight, skill, knowledge and discipline. I don't invest where I lose all control or don't fully understand the risk.

If trading were as simple as buying *low* and selling *high*, everyone would be retired, young and mortgage-free.

Greed Instead of Need Makes Us Foolish - Not Wise

Many people after a few wins believe they've cracked the code to be a successful trader or a successful entrepreneur. If this sounds familiar you may already feel invincible. But success has a shelf-life. Maximising today is vital in business as none of us knows what tomorrow brings. Here are three sobering stories of *smart* friends who forgot that at some point if we keep driving with our foot down, we will run out of petrol. Two of them never needed to work again for money.

The Consultant and Day Trader

After 15 years of consistent profitable trading in stocks, he lost 80% of his capital in a single day. He made a bet that was not properly hedged and the market went against him.

The Crypto Millionaire

A full-time crypto trader who built up a substantial portfolio over a decade. Overtraded. Overconfident. Lost it all. Millions of dollars gone.

The Entrepreneur

A successful entrepreneur for forty years. Financially secure. Able to retire. He invested millions into his new business, expecting to multiply his wealth 50-fold. He kept waiting on the *promised* big deals to drop. His addiction to the dazzling lights of *guaranteed* financial success, were nothing more than an illusion - one that convinced him to sink more and more money into the business. The venture never got off the ground. He was left with 250 euros in the bank.

All are over 55. Their decisions didn't just affect them, but their families too. Be consciously careful and mindful of the risks versus imaginary rewards.

The Moral of The Story

Success Doesn't Last Forever

Greed and foolishness create havoc in our lives.

People who forever chase success rarely catch it. It's easy to get addicted and high on the constant need for success. As soon as we believe our own smoke and mirrors and that we are untouchable, the universe has a habit of giving us a harsh lesson. Where you are today, financially, emotionally and mentally, is the sum of your decisions.

I've always kept life simple. My first goal? To own my home, mortgage-free. No matter what happens, I'll always have a roof over my head. Remember, once the mortgage is paid off, every mortgage payment you paid out (after tax) becomes your monthly savings.

Some of you may believe it's better to rent and use your excess capital to invest instead. Paying rent forever isn't my idea of certainty for the future - to have a constant outgoing for a basic need until the end of life. I prefer a home to live in, rent and mortgage-free. Nor is investing when the outcome is based on big promises. Either way, make your choice but *be careful out there*!

If you invest in stocks or crypto, risk what you can afford to lose. Yes - lose. It's a gamble.

Not even Warren Buffet knows what will happen tomorrow. Keeping this perspective will force you to pause, reflect and ask:

Do I really know what I am doing?

Top Tips From The Trading Floor

As a bond trader, I observed that successful traders took small profits along the way. If you are fortunate to double or substantially increase your investment, consider recouping your investment and continue trading with the profits.

My boss gave me three golden rules which have stuck with me:

1. It's never wrong to take a profit.
2. Take a loss early. The first cut is always the cheapest.
3. Don't be greedy. Always leave a profit for the next person.

Over time, life reveals to us undeniable truths. A few of these truths are more brutal than others...

☆ Never make the same mistake twice.
☆ Mistakes are made so we can correct ourselves.

☆ It's always cheaper to learn from other people's mistakes.
☆ Smart people make fewer mistakes.
☆ Smart people minimise risk.
☆ Unintelligent people hope for the best.
☆ Success demands motivation, preparation and careful execution.
☆ Consider the value of your hard-earned cash. Every pound, dollar or euro you spend represents not just money, but time and tax already paid - before it ever reaches your pocket.
☆ Simplicity is the secret to success.

Summary

If your desire for success never ends, you will never be content.

If your only goal is accumulation, you will never be free.

Freedom and wisdom are yours to grab and keep.

Discover and fulfil your meaningful purpose.

Keep your integrity firmly intact.

Be the example to the world. *Go for It!*

"Not everything that counts can be counted, and not everything that can be counted counts." Attributed to Albert Einstein.

MOTIVATION ZONE

The Power of Success

Success isn't only about reaching your goals - it's about evolving into your own power with grace, generosity and wisdom. I'm convinced that when we do our work with a conscious attitude, success is rewarding both financially and spiritually - not only for us, but for others too.

By my mid-thirties, my income increased exponentially. As I meditated more, a thought came to me.

I can share my success with others who need a helping hand.

That thought embedded a deeper meaning to my ambition.

Just double-checking - are you reading this in *Zen Button* mode? The quieter the mind, the more we absorb.

I chose small charities that really needed help - centred around education - because the kids have to do the work. I trusted my inner voice and kept my business antenna on, to ensure money was spent wisely and it was actually needed. I gave spontaneously and as privately as possible. And I noticed something remarkable. Even when I gave away 10% of my salary, my income the following year always surpassed the previous year's donations. This happened consistently year after year.

How does that work?

The act of giving benefits the donor financially as much as the charity! Isn't that incredible? The universe really does provide in mysterious ways. *And*, the pleasure of giving is just as amazing for the giver as the receiver. In a famous Buddhist scripture, the Lotus Sutra, it is said that an enlightened being, a *bodhisattva* "gives not to acquire merit, but because giving is the nature of an awakened heart."

Summary

This gives us a clue about *happy, meaningful success*. It's not just about personal gain. When we give joyfully with an open heart, financially or otherwise, everyone benefits. As Mother Teresa reminds us, "It's not how much we give but how much love we put into giving."

Your Turn

Change tactics - Make the Mind your Servant

What does financial freedom mean to you?

Who can you give a helping hand to financially or with your time?

You're Chasing your Dreams but You're Not Fulfilled

✧ You feel	Worn out. You've hit a crossroads in your career.
✧ You tell yourself	*I have to keep pushing. Maybe I missed my chance. If I slow down I could lose my job.*
✧ Flip the Switch	*I'm going to calmly anchor myself in the flow of the moment. Eyes closed, I watch the life-force gently flow in and out of my nose – connecting fully with my true state of being. I'll make time in my schedule daily to rebuild my positivity. Clarity, not fear will guide my actions. No pressure. I've got this.*

You've Dug Yourself into a Financial Hole

❖ **You feel** — There's no way out. The bills keep piling up.

❖ **You tell Yourself** — *I can't pay my debts. I could lose everything. I have to now face my reality.*

❖ **Flip the Switch** — *I've overcome problems before and I will do it now. Every problem has a solution. I will take positive steps and advice to repair my situation and face the truth head on. I will explain my difficulties confidently and honestly with my creditors and negotiate manageable terms. I am not afraid. I'm not ashamed. I'm learning. I'm moving forward. I'm ready to learn and change. I'll not give up or feel sorry for myself. Something good will come.*

Your Career is Stagnant

❖ **You feel** — Overwhelmed and unappreciated.

❖ **You tell yourself** — *I work hard but don't see any progress. Perhaps I'm not cut out for this anymore.*

❖ **Flip the Switch** — *I'm proud of my achievements. I am more than my job title. I don't need to measure myself against others. I'll give myself space to reflect to find what's the best path ahead. If my heart no longer feels aligned with my work, I will explore new options, slowly and methodically. I trust myself fully.*

CHANGE TACTICS - REIGNITE YOUR PURPOSE

☆ Write down a new pledge to re-centre your work with what matters to you
☆ List how you can streamline your work. Delegate better? Prioritize?

Invest In Yourself

Spend just an hour a day learning something new that excites you. Nothing to do with work.

I have every confidence in you! Celebrate even the smallest wins.

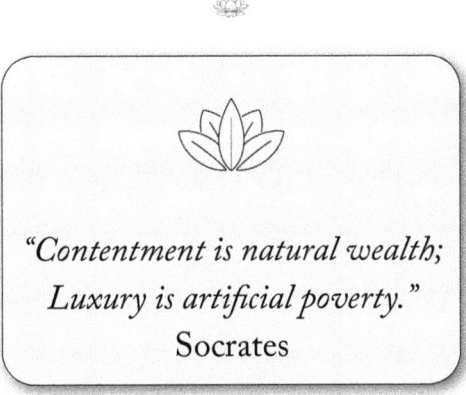

"*Contentment is natural wealth;*
Luxury is artificial poverty."
Socrates

NOTES

PART SIX

SELF-AWARENESS
PERSONAL GROWTH & HEALTH

Optimise your Wellbeing

SELF-AWARENESS
PERSONAL GROWTH & HEALTH

In Part Six, we start with exploring self awareness with more snippets from my silence challenge. Then the secret wisdom continues on a range of subjects - how to live consciously, bullying, negative thoughts, veganism and finally my secret recipe for what might just be the best hummus on the planet! You now know the drill! More questions to ask yourself in Contemplation Corner. I'm sure if this were an exam you'd score A+. Then we will reflect on happiness and the power of smiling. Motivation Zone offers you the chance to take the ultimate selfie of truth - to assess your personal consciousness balance sheet.

We've covered a great deal of ground. Hopefully, you're already discovering a fresh perspective on how you want to experience life, connect and be. Are you *feeling* more in tune with the *real* you?

I recently came across the American motivational speaker and writer Jim Rohn. He made two stand-out observations about self-development. He said, "Don't wish it were easier, wish you were better," and, "If you don't like how things are, change it! You're not a tree."

We've already discussed taking ownership and responsibility and the importance of regenerating our self-worth, knowledge, thoughts and actions, to build a concrete foundation for reaching our goals. In other words, the fundamentals all need to work together in harmony and not against each other. Now we'll explore how to live more consciously, how to confront our inner and outer enemies, rethink our diet and reflect on our mindset around money. Practical wisdom and gentle challenges to build self-awareness, resilience and a healthy, happy life.

Health is more than green smoothies and gym selfies. It's about how you treat yourself - what you feed your mind and stomach through your eyes, mouth and ears. Everything you 'eat' influences your emotional, mental and physical health.

Self-Awareness in Silence

My silence challenge could be described as a self-awareness expedition into the unknown. I was confronted and sometimes soothed by the patterns, habits and beliefs which had been operating inside of me since birth. Silence reveals that most of us hide under the surface, reacting to circumstances rather than creating what we want and feeling our truth.

Self-awareness isn't another technique. It's the foundation on which to build a happy, meaningful life - to trust the knowledge and wisdom that life gives us. It's the moment to explore new territories of consciousness and heal old wounds.

During my silence, healthy self-awareness, inner growth and keeping physically and mentally fit, were key to my survival. Self-awareness isn't about perfection or endlessly attending self-improvement courses every other week - it's about honestly seeing what YOU really want and making conscious choices that support your wellbeing and health.

* * * SILENCE DIARY EXTRACT * * *

Day 27

"2.18 am. *It can't be that early! Am I supposed to get up?* Went to bed last night at 10pm. I'm now down to four-and-a-half hours sleep. Six is my norm. Must be all the power from meditating so much. I feel great. Sounds like it's raining. Ankle hurts. I get up. Put coconut oil on it. No bruise. Arnica would be better but I don't have any. Exercises. Nineteen press-ups. Not bad for this time of the day!"

[Even getting up this early, I stick to my stretching routine which is a mix of stretching, Yoga and Pilates]

Meditate for around four hours. It's beautiful to meditate and then slowly becoming aware of nature waking up around us with the birds singing. Feeling relaxed. My head seems to have expanded into emptiness. Hard to describe the feeling. I sit outside on the balcony and relax with my eyes closed. Silence.

Later I make Dr Shinya's simple, high-enzyme concoction of apple, spinach and lemon blended. It's amazingly refreshing."

[I kept a note of everything I cooked. This drink is a tonic booster from Dr Hiromi Shinya, the famous gastroenterologist.]

"Meditate for another hour outside. I make a fresh broccoli and courgette soup. Delicious! Body strong, mind good. Perfect.

I wonder, *'Am I the prisoner in the castle or are the real prisoners in the outside world?'* Outsiders would surely say I am the prisoner with a limited, strict, boring regime devoid of external stimulation. But, really, who is freer?

I have picked up a routine which subtly shifts - we spend our lives on the same bus or train, walk up the same street to work, have the same sandwich for lunch, follow the same routine coming home. It's *life* and we have responsibilities to meet. But if the routine lacks any spiritual inlet then how will we ever be free? What's for sure is the simpler we keep our lives, the more freedom we have."

* * *

Silence heightened my awareness of every feeling, thought and action. On reflection, I now see the experience today as an experiment that shaped a holistic framework for my own personal growth and to share with others.

YOUR TURN

As an idea, choose a single routine like cooking dinner, and perform it without any distraction, consciously. Note down the experience - your feelings, thoughts and emotions. Try it for a week. This simple exercise will show you how your mind shifts, and how you become in rhythm with your true nature of calmness, peace and stillness.

Are you fully present in the flow of the moment or on autopilot? Fancy a quick meditation before going to the next secret? Go for it. Three minutes is all you need to replenish your energy.

SECRET #35

HOW TO LIVE A CONSCIOUS LIFE
one moment at a time

The secret wisdom whispers in your ear

Are we living a meaningful life?

Chill out for a moment, my friend
Stop what you are doing
Take a moment to just relax
Enjoy a conscious breath
And another
Each breath is a gift
Be conscious of the life-force in each breath

Remember

Our lives are hanging by a delicate thread
We are nothing more than a speck of stardust in the infinite universe
Life is a spiritual journey encouraging us...holding us...guiding us...
To consciousness and freedom
We can choose to live with consciousness and awareness or live in ignorance and false bliss

Life is a privilege
Appreciate its rarity
Everything in the world is impermanent

The body will die, yet we act as if we will live forever

Do you want to live a life of Calmness?

...a life of Peace?

...a life of Happiness?

Do you ever even ask these questions or care about the answers?

Everything is possible if you are prepared to create the happiness you *really* want

Everything becomes possible when you master the mind...

...when you stop to ask and realise fully the highest goals of life...

What am I doing? What is my purpose? What makes me happy?

A conscious person...

...lives in truth...

...becomes the contemplating witness

...accepts life and what it brings

...never gives away their power to others

...laughs at life

A conscious person...

...knows when to speak and when to stay silent

...only pays attention to thoughts which have value

...remains positive with the knowledge that difficulties pass

A conscious person practises inner stillness

A kind of *mindlessness*

A state of no thoughts

When you have fewer thoughts, you spend more time feeling positive and less time being negative

Conscious, successful people are the humblest people

Humble people serve the world faithfully

Meaningful success is the manifestation of our noble desires

Living a life of restlessness creates endless desires...

...for power and influence

...to accumulate and show off wealth

...to buy more bricks and mortar

...to dress to impress

Living a conscious life allows your silent power inside to manifest into reality

My friend, think deeply and honestly

Are you kind to yourself?

Do you choose the path of the righteous which encompasses a meaningful life and meaningful success?

Conscious people also enjoy the fruits of their labour but these fruits do not create endless desires or selfishness

Who really wants to live a conscious life?

MINDFUL THOUGHTS
ON LIVING A CONSCIOUS LIFE

Making the same mistakes repeatedly will not help you be successful, calm, peaceful and happy.

Empower yourself with effective self-analysis.

Consider how many of your thoughts and words are meaningful and how many are meaningless?

Conscious people actively alter their reactions, actions, thoughts and behaviour.

Negative thoughts have one purpose. To challenge and defeat them!

Remember:

Self-analysis is not self-criticism.

Consciousness, empowerment and inner stillness all begin with self-awareness. Self-awareness can be awakened through meditation, mindfulness and silent reflection. The way we respond to and face others, even those who mistreat or challenge us, reflects how we feel deeply inside about ourselves.

SECRET #36

HOW TO DEAL WITH BULLIES
by increasing your self-esteem

The secret wisdom whispers in your ear

A person with high self-esteem and kindness will never bully

A person with low self-esteem or low confidence is more likely to be bullied

A person with high self-esteem or high confidence is unlikely to be bullied

A person with low self-esteem, arrogance and power is more likely to be a bully

Each of us has the power to be humble or to misuse our power to bully

Each of us has the power to resist and stand up to a bully

Self-awareness and self-confidence are key to repel the bully

Bullies are like predators

Bullies *test* the water and observe the reaction to decide whether to continue

Bullies are weak and feed off our weaknesses...but are repelled by our strength

Bullies continue unless we stand up to them

The bully has limited power over us unless we grant them full power

The bully has no right to treat us like a *nobody* unless we allow it

The bully is full of insecurity, selfishness, anger, cruelty and self-importance

The answers to life are so often found in nature

Watch the animals, my friend
The lion scans the herd
Smells the fear
And seeks the easy kill
The lion waits for the moment and then pounces
The lion *never* attacks the strongest and fastest
Instead
The lion targets the most vulnerable
The lion attacks the weakest prey
The bully also attacks the weakest target

How can we turn weakness into strength?
Inner weakness and fear encourages the bully
Inner strength and action deters the bully
Stand up and resist without fear
Confronting a bully is the last thing a bully expects
Every bully will meet their destiny one day

Tap into your inner power
Meditate and feel that strength and protection inside and
around you
Be clear
Be strong

Changing your behaviour changes your energy
If the bullying continues, surround yourself with strength
The longer it goes on, the weaker you become
The quicker you stand up, the stronger you become

Find a strong ally to help you find the courage to confront the bully

Who wants to deal with the bully?

MINDFUL THOUGHTS ON DEALING WITH BULLIES

Don't take abuse from anybody. Don't give away your power.
Stay calm.

Increasing your mental and physical power will deter negative
people automatically and attract positive people.

Showing your vulnerability and being open emotionally is a
positive trait only in the right environment. Put out the fire
when it's just a spark.

Remember the encouraging words of Eleanor Roosevelt:

"No one can make you feel inferior without your consent."

MEANINGFUL PROMPT

Think about someone you admire who is strong. What would
they do in your shoes if they were in your situation?

BREATH AWARENESS

In times of stress, take three slow breaths and mentally create a
positive shield of energy around you.

VISUALISATION

Imagine a golden shield around you repelling all negatives.
With every conscious breath, the field is reinforced.

SECRET #37

HOW TO AVOID NEGATIVE THOUGHTS
that drag you down

The secret wisdom whispers in your ear

Is the empty glass *really* empty?
The glass that appears empty is full of air
The half-full glass is *really* full - half-full of liquid and half-full of air
Is the glass *actually* a glass or something else?
The glass is *actually just* sand, silica, air, limestone and heat

Is our mind full, half-full or empty?
As we think, so we are

What happens when we feel negative?

Negative thoughts make us see, feel and experience negativity everywhere
Negative thoughts...
...make us lose faith
...make us tired and confused
...can encourage self-harm and self-sabotage
Negative thoughts encourage laziness and waste our energy
Negative thoughts destroy time and motivation

What enters the mind and body affects our thoughts and our state of being
We all have the choice to listen to truth or listen to lies

We all have the choice to consume what is healthy or unhealthy

When we feel depressed, we eat unhealthy food and indulge in unhealthy habits

When we feel depressed, we don't want to hear truth

How we think about ourselves is who we become

What we become is who we are

What we do and think today will influence who we are tomorrow

My friend, the good news is that being negative is a choice you can change in an instant

To avoid negative thoughts, steer clear of people who feed your doubts

To be successful, avoid negative thinking

Positive people overwhelm negative thoughts with a cheerful outlook

The good news is that the answers to your problems often have the simplest solutions

Remember the KISS motto

Keep It Simple Stupid

To attract positivity, hang out with positive people

Positive people influence our mood and boost our confidence

When we think positively we can help...

...negative people who need our support and love

...negative people who need a helping hand

...negative people who need us to make them laugh

Who wants to avoid negativity?

MINDFUL THOUGHTS ON HOW TO AVOID NEGATIVE THOUGHTS

"Negative people need drama like oxygen. Stay positive, it will take their breath away." Unknown

Meditation helps us to be more positive and surf above the waves of negative thoughts

Keep good company inside and outside.

When surrounded by negative people, keep the energy positive inside.

When surrounded by negative people, change your phone number.

When surrounded by moaners and groaners, leave the room.

Have a quick look in the mirror to double-check you're not one of them!

REFLECTION

Reflect on a habit, person or place that triggers negativity. What's one change you could make to avoid this happening again?

SECRET #38

HOW TO SPEND MONEY CONSCIOUSLY
to retire young and be free

The secret wisdom whispers in your ear

Should we flash the cash or keep a stash?
That is the question
Should we save or should we rave?

Should we spend our cash on metal and rubber?
On designer clothes?
On expensive meals?
Should we gamble our cash on invisible crypto flying in the clouds?

What do we love the most, need the most, crave the most?
What do we *need* to live a life of contentment?

Mind over matter is all that matters
What matters the most is our health
And being surrounded by love
What matters the most is being free...
...sleeping safely at night
...being able to eat today
...breathing fresh air today

A person who earns money honestly, spends money consciously

A person who earns money deviously, spends money unconsciously

Too much money is dangerous in the wrong hands

Too much money can increase...

...ego, pride and vanity

...arrogance and selfishness

Too much money can...

...reduce our values and empathy for others

...corrupt us and our family

...reduce our humility

...blind us with fake power

Spare some cash for others...

...who need it

...who will use it well

...for those we love

...for having fun

...for a rainy day

Save more cash to retire early

Who wants to spend money consciously?

MINDFUL THOUGHTS
ON SPENDING MONEY CONSCIOUSLY

Avoid being trapped in an invisible spiral of debt, stress and financial bondage. Enjoy the freedom money gives.

BUT today's financial success doesn't guarantee financial success tomorrow.

Be careful.

If you are twenty, consider saving at least 10% of your salary every month

If you are thirty, consider saving at least 20% of your salary every month

If you are forty, consider saving at least 30% of your salary every month

Living a life of contentment is better than living a life of temporary extravagance.

Stay humble. Stay free. Stay balanced. Stay content. Take responsibility.

THE BIG SECRET to financial freedom isn't about wanting more and more, but about wanting less and less.

ACTION

Set a savings goal for next month. Keep half and treat yourself with the other half. Repeat if it feels motivational and worthwhile.

SECRET #39

HOW TO LIVE IN TRUTH
when everyone else is telling porky pies

The secret wisdom whispers in your ear

What is truth?

Who is living in truth?

Can we live *our* truth

...in a world of impermanence, intolerance and intransigence?

...in a world of smoke and mirrors?

...in a world where few have the courage to be truthful?

Or do we prefer to live blindly in a world of delusion and confusion?

We are creatures of habit...

...but are we creatures of ethical habits?

We are creatures of imagination...

...but will imagination manifest our true path?

So many questions, but what is the answer to find our truth?

The path of truth is a narrow path...

...a path few have the backbone to follow

...a path few will ever tread

...a path very few believe even exists

Step One is to STOP and CONTEMPLATE...

What am I doing, am I happy, am I peaceful or am I suffering?

Step Two is to START to BE TRUTHFUL with ourselves!

Do you want to be amongst the few or lost in the crowd?

The path of the masses is *unconscious* living...
...meaningless thoughts
...meaningless chit-chat
...meaningless fears and doubts
...meaningless meetings
...meaningless projections of the person you want to be...
...instead of the beautiful person you already ARE...

The path of the few is to find our true nature
...to find our meaning
...to find real joy

My sweetest friend...
...if it ain't working, fix it
...if it ain't broke, don't fix it
...the courageous and sincere find meaningful success
...the courageous and sincere manifest a vibrant life

To change your mindset, you have to change your habits...
...healthy habits make your mind and body healthy
To change your habits, you have to break old patterns of
negativity and sorrow...
...negativity and sorrow can be overcome with light and
positive power
To change is to live with a smile
To conform is to live with misery

To stand still with negative thoughts will sink all of us further from truth

Who wants to live in truth?

MINDFUL THOUGHTS ON HOW TO LIVE IN TRUTH

"Truth is like the sun. You can shut it away for a time, but it ain't going away." Elvis Presley.

Wishing your life were better will change nothing.

Wishing you had a better job or a better partner will change nothing.

Wishing your life away with fantasy will change nothing.

A recent Oracle study showed that nearly 90% of people are looking for more experiences to help them smile and laugh. Forty-five percent have not felt true happiness in the past two years and 25% have forgotten what happiness really is.

Happiness and truth will set you free.

CONTEMPLATION CORNER

☆ Consciousness ☆ Bullies ☆ Negative ☆
☆ Thoughts ☆ Save and Spend ☆ Truth ☆

At school most of us gave a punch and received a punch along the way without becoming serial bullies or being badly bullied. You may have sadly suffered much more.

Wise people use forgiveness as a powerful tool to heal the past. A yogic technique to purify the past is to see memories in the mind as a library of books. We do not deny that all of the books exist in the library of the mind, but it's our choice which books we choose to read. Luckily, the past does not determine our future and the past does not have to repeat.

DECIDE HERE AND NOW HOW YOU'RE GOING TO ADD MORE CALMNESS IN YOUR LIFE. Calmness leads to more consciousness. To be in tune with what you really want.

HOW ABOUT FROM TOMORROW BEING MORE CONSCIOUS BY IGNORING YOUR NEGATIVE THOUGHTS? Write down your empowering, positive thoughts. Repeat daily.

HOW MUCH MONEY ARE YOU GOING TO SET ASIDE MONTHLY FOR THE NEXT SIX MONTHS AND EVERY MONTH? WHAT HABIT DON'T YOU NEED ANYMORE TO ACHIEVE THIS?

*Nothing changes if we keep
making the same old excuses
Change the music!*

SECRET #40

HOW TO BE A HEALTHY VEGAN
without eating rabbit food

The secret wisdom whispers in your ear

Being a humble vegan is to respect the choice of others

Being vegan is...
...a lifestyle choice
...a wonderful way to create a balanced life
...a natural step to being more healthy

Being vegan, it's important to consume protein with each meal
It helps to know how to cook
It's sensible to vary the protein
Being vegan can lead to an unhealthy lifestyle of too many
carbs and processed food...
and too many brownies!

Healthy vegans...
...eat organic seeds, nuts and pulses for protein
...choose organic, fresh food and avoid processed food
...when using supplements, choose naturally derived, plant-
based vitamins
Healthy vegans follow a sattvic diet

Sattva is the Sanskrit word for goodness, purity, balance,
peacefulness, truth and positivity

A *sattvic* diet is a diet based on fresh fruit, fresh vegetables and whole grains

A *sattvic* diet is a balanced diet...

...leads to a balanced mind

A *sattvic* diet has the right balance of carbs and protein

Who wants to be a healthy vegan?

MINDFUL THOUGHTS ON
BEING A HEALTHY VEGAN

Eating plant-based food is a fantastic way to contribute to saving the planet. Try it full or part-time.

According to the UN Food and Agriculture Organization, vegans help reduce 15% of the world's global greenhouse gas emissions. That's more than every car, train and plane put together.

Eating plant-based food is also great for your health.

A recent umbrella study, published in the Public Library of Science (Plos) journal, analysed 23 years of multiple peer-reviewed studies on the health of vegans and vegetarians. The study concluded that vegans and vegetarians have lower blood pressure, less obesity, less heart disease and less cancer, with multiple positive health-indicators compared to normal diets.

How about adapting a 5:2 vegan diet (5 days vegan, 2 days non-vegan), a 2:5 vegan diet or a 4:3 vegan diet each week?

REFLECTION

Whatever you choose to eat, before your next meal, consider pausing for a moment with gratefulness. Think about how the food arrived on your plate and the amazing people who made it possible.

SECRET #41

HOW TO MAKE THE BEST HUMMUS
on the planet

The secret wisdom whispers in your ear

Hummus is full of protein and micronutrients
Hummus transports our imagination to the desert
Living like nomads in a tent without a care in the world

Make hummus not war

Make hummus with kalamata olives - a great combination
Make hummus as follows:
Take 250g of dried organic chickpeas
Take a saucepan and cover in cold water for 24 hours
Take a colander, thoroughly rinse the chickpeas
Fill a saucepan with fresh boiling water and add the chickpeas
Add a heaped teaspoon of organic vegan bouillon to the hot water
Partially cover with a lid and gently boil for one hour
Add more boiling water as needed
Allow to cool down
Keep the stock
Keep your patience, the result is worthwhile
Once cool, add the chickpeas to the blender
Now is THE BIG SECRET
Add the water that cooked the chickpeas with the stock

Use enough to cover the chickpeas
Add a little more if needed later

Enjoy meditating whilst the chickpeas are simmering

Add the following...
a teaspoon of tahini; one organic squeezed lemon
three tablespoons of chopped kalamata olives
two tablespoons of extra-virgin olive oil
more olive oil as needed
Check the taste and texture
Add salt if needed or soy sauce
Yes, soy sauce! Asian confusion! It works

Enjoy with crackers
Enjoy being crackers

Who really wants to make the best hummus on the planet?

MINDFUL THOUGHTS ON HUMMUS

Hummus is packed with nutrients like choline, magnesium, vitamin B6, all of which support memory, mood and mental clarity. The Cleveland Clinic carried out studies which show chickpeas support steady blood sugar levels, heart health and gut balance. These studies were published in the peer-reviewed journals of MDPI.

Chef's warning...under-soaking or under-cooking the chickpeas could lead to unintended consequences... and being kicked out of the bedroom by the dog!

SECRET #42

HOW TO STOP EATING ANIMALS
whilst stroking your favourite pet

The secret wisdom whispers in your ear

Can we justify taking another life?
If it moves, it breathes
If it moves, it has life
If it moves, it feels

Life is precious
Life is beautiful if we eat from the land
If we eat meat, we are eating a living being
If we eat fish, we are eating a living being
If we eat chicken, we are eating a living being

What do you see on your plate when you eat?

Who *really* can say they are friends to all the beautiful animals in the world?

Who wants to stop eating animals?

MINDFUL THOUGHTS ON
HOW TO STOP EATING ANIMALS

There's a reason why none of us lives next to the abattoir.
When you munch on your bacon butty, contemplate what you are eating.

Scientific studies show that pigs are as intelligent as dogs.

Did you ever wonder if the food on your plate died in fear?

Jeremy Bentham, a British philosopher in the 18th century commented, "The question is not, can they reason? Nor, can they talk? But can they suffer?"

TRY THIS

Swap one animal product for a plant-based alternative this week. If it feels good, keep going.

REFLECTION

How does your choice of food correlate with your values?

"Let food be thy medicine and medicine be thy food."
Hippocrates, well-known Greek physician and philosopher.

CONTEMPLATION CORNER

☆ Veganism ☆ Animals ☆

Socrates, who was a vegetarian, reminded us to live in our own truth. George Bernard Shaw, Nobel Peace Prize Winner for literature, was derided when he attended a dinner party for only eating salad. He told the laughing audience, "my stomach is not a graveyard for dead animals."

Gandhi, Einstein, St Francis of Assisi were all vegans. Today's celebrities reported to be vegan include Lewis Hamilton, Ariana Grande, Madonna, Venus Williams, Brian May, Will.i.am, Stevie Wonder and Novak Djokovic.

Cambridge University Press reports an estimated 125 billion fish and an estimated 80 billion mammals and birds are killed for food each year. We throw away 30% of the food produced. That means sixty billion fish and animals die unnecessarily each year. Read that again.

Close your eyes. Stop. Feel. Think.

As a minimum, even if we keep our diets intact, society should stop wasting the life of animals. I'm genuinely not here to preach about what you should eat. But valuing nature's resources is surely a win-win for the environment, nature, our family and friends and future generations.

Choose a diet that makes you feel healthy and full of energy, that makes effective use of our planet's resources. Cooking healthy, fresh food is the way to go. Try ditching the microwave and ready-made meals.

What are you prepared to do to make your diet healthier? How about trying a few vegan or vegetarian recipes for fun?

READY TO CHANGE SOMETHING ABOUT YOURSELF OR TRY SOMETHING NEW?

ARE YOU LIVING YOUR TRUTH? HOW CAN YOU ACHIEVE THE HAPPY, MEANINGFUL SUCCESS YOU DESERVE?

Truth = Happiness?
Or
Truth = Unhappiness?

Be honest.
If you are told the truth, are you grateful or angry?

REFLECTIONS

What Do You Want?

Living our truth is the essential ingredient for happiness - integrating peace, love and contentment between mind, body and spirit.

I was brought up with the simple mantra that I could have 'whatever I wanted if I wanted it enough.' No ifs, no buts. I believed it. Naïve, definitely - but I had a strong will and desire to learn. I had no doubt. That belief *drove me* to career success. It can surely drive you also to where you want to go.

What I wasn't told about was the physical, mental and emotional stress we have to go through to succeed. Meditation became my number one *healthy,* effective daily rescue remedy at the height of my career.

Overcoming Adversity

One of the worst forms of torture is removing a person's liberty when they have done nothing wrong. I discovered very recently that my grandfather was a war hero in the Resistance. He was arrested by the Gestapo in October 1942. Vilified and subjected to a demeaning daily roulette of life or death, *he survived!*

After the war, he spent one year in hospital. Emaciated, riddled with disease. Just 37kg.

And still, he survived.

My grandfather had risky major heart surgery when he was fifty. *He survived!*

In spite of his horrific past experiences, he found strength, courage and love. He never gave up. He later lived a long, fulfilling, happy life.

My grandfather's heartwarming story reminds us that resilience is built on survival. The will to keep going no matter the odds. I hope it encourages you to be strong in adversity, to help you overcome the difficulties of the past, what troubles you now and to create a meaningful future. Regardless of what difficulties we are facing, someone else is facing far worse problems.

Problems & Mistakes

When I was a kid, my dad bought me a huge eraser which said, "I never make big misteaks!"

I hated making mistakes - but each mistake just made me more determined to do better next time. A reminder that mistakes are made to correct ourselves - as feedback not failure. I always accept and admire anyone who is far more talented than me. I often think to myself, *What can I learn from that person to help me improve?* Do you adopt a similar approach?

Effort and determination always outperform raw talent in the end. It's also smart to learn from our own experiences. For example, many people have a dry January, feel and sleep great and then on 1st February start drinking again. What's the sense of making the effort if you throw away the gains a month later?

Attitude

If we walk along all day searching for sympathy, thinking, *I'm a failure, I'm unhappy, I'm depressed, nobody loves me, I'm overweight,* how can that help us? The cumulative effect is we will not enjoy life and dislike ourselves.

I get it! When life's not going our way, we all need a shoulder to cry on. But being caught up in a never-ending maze of negativity is the path to nowhere. I make no apology for the repetition of positive vibes, words and thoughts. I keep emphasising the need for us to be positive, truthful, happy, and healthy. Incremental changes in our life lead to steady, *happy, meaningful success*. So often we repeat what makes us unhappy, instead of adjusting our short-term goals to something achievable.

One of the keys to realising the message of *The Big Secret of How* is remembering to take your *Selfie of Truth* now and again, to check-in with yourself - to make your tomorrow spectacular instead of average.

To succeed, focus on the goal and not the sacrifice.

1) Focus on the mini-successes and not the mini-failures.
   It's too easy to see what's wrong instead of what's right.
2) Concentrate on what you know - instead of stressing about what you don't know.
   Accentuate your positives and improve your weaknesses with half an hour of self-study each day to help you improve.
3) Turbo-charge your attitude so that every small act becomes successful.
   Making the best coffee in the office, asking questions with enthusiasm and striving to improve yourself daily will boost your confidence and the confidence others have in you.

Tiny shifts initiate tidal waves of change.

You Can Do It

As you know already, gratitude, humility and contentment are the benefits of *happy, meaningful success*. You don't have to spend your life chasing a never-ending dream, stuck in a job you don't love, feeling lonely or unhappy, spending money you don't have on things you don't need, or trapping yourself in an invisible cage - hoping one day to be free.

You have the power to alter how you think and how you respond.

You *can* break free from the endless *law* of cause and effect - by finding your purpose.

If I can do it, so can you. Your next life chapter begins with one brave decision - one honest moment of truth.

It's yours for the taking - if you want it enough, you can have whatever you want.

No excuses.

Go For It!

MOTIVATION ZONE

Which Technique is Best for Personal Growth?

Once upon a time there was a fox and a cat living on the edge of a forest. They were good friends. They lived in fear that one day the wild dogs would attack them from the other side of the forest. The fox had a notebook. Every idea he wrote down. New escape routes, new methods to avoid being attacked, in fact, so many, that he had a whole book full of options. The dreaded day came. The cat knew only one technique. It ran quickly up a branch near the top of the tree. The fox was busy looking at his notebook for the best plan in spite of his friend pleading for him to run up the tree. Too late. The fox's indecision cost him dearly.

Growing our knowledge and staying curious are key motivators to remain enthusiastic and fresh in our pursuit of *happy, meaningful success.* Whichever techniques you use for personal growth, study and test them, preferably one at a time. Become an expert. Find a teacher you love and respect. Follow and practise. Remember it took me five years of daily meditation to make it as natural as getting up in the morning. And I was disciplined! Meditation techniques are designed to take you to stillness and calmness. Success is guaranteed if you keep going and keep growing. The slowest marathon runner will certainly reach the finish line. It may take longer than the fastest, but so what! The quitters never make the finish line. The same can be said about affirmations and other techniques. They have one purpose. To remember our true nature - to be content, successful and healthy. All-round development is essential. It's no good sorting out our career without paying attention to our health and our relationships. This is why we've covered so many topics.

I encourage you to choose what works for you and what motivates you. We cannot proceed if we are demotivated.

Self-Awareness

Improving self-awareness is one of the biggest blind spots to overcome. We often take feedback as criticism, think we smile more than we do, and crucially, underestimate how negative we are without realising it. Resistance to change drains away our energy, and perfectionism is an illusion that holds us back.

THE BIG SECRET is to realise that true power manifests when you take full ownership and accountability of the present moment. The best way to take responsibility is to go beyond writing a list of excuses of the past and owning every event in your life. Put yourself at the top of the list for every failure and give thanks for every success. Change starts only when we recognise the truth of the past.

The Science of Smiling

Once I carried out an experiment on a waitress. I popped in to a café for a cuppa a few times a week and noticed that the waitress never smiled. We all have bad days but surely not every day, month in, month out, when part of the job is to be friendly. It didn't matter how often I smiled at her, even adding extra helpings of British politeness, she never smiled back. Her demeanour was the same to everyone. I wondered if it was cultural - she was from Eastern Europe. Still, I persevered, curious if a breakthrough would come. One day, I saw her laughing and chatting with a colleague for the first time. When I paid the bill I said, "You have a beautiful smile." She smiled back at me and always smiled at me after that moment.

Scientific studies show that smiling increases activity in the brain including...

...the amygdala, the area of the brain which processes our emotions;

...the prefrontal cortex, linked to mood regulation.

Smiling releases ...

Dopamine	*the natural fuel to make us motivated and happy;*
Serotonin	*enhances our feelings of well-being; and*
Endorphins	*natural painkillers and mood-enhancers.*

What's not to like?

Try This Mood-Shifter Experiment!

Tomorrow, consciously smile at every person you pass in the street. Notice how your mood changes, especially when they smile back. Smiling is contagious. It radiates happiness - and when we are smiling we are receptive and open.

Your Personal Consciousness Balance Sheet

Are you ready for extra self-analysis? Earlier, you did a snapshot of your financial position.

I've dreamed up a *personal consciousness balance sheet* - your big moment to take a *High Definition 360° Selfie of Truth* - to gauge your self awareness and level of consciousness.

Grab a pen. Don't take it too seriously - but do be completely honest. Use it as a benchmark to highlight areas for improvement. Be spontaneous and intuitive. Be conscious. Think for no more than 30 seconds on each topic and mark yourself with a score between one and ten.

On the left, under assets, 10 is the highest score, 0 is the lowest. On the right, under liabilities, -10 is the lowest score and 0 is the 'highest' score.

MY TRUE PERSONAL BALANCE SHEET

ASSETS	LIABILITIES
CURRENT ASSETS	**CURRENT LIABILITIES**

ASSETS		LIABILITIES	
PAST CONDITIONING	_____	PAST CONDITIONING	_____
PHYSICAL HEALTH/DIET	_____	LAZINESS/BAD ATTITUDE	_____
MENTAL HEALTH	_____	MENTAL HEALTH	_____
EMOTIONAL HEALTH	_____	UNHEALTHY LIFESTYLE	_____
HAPPINESS/	_____	UNHAPPINESS/FEAR/WORRY	_____
FAITH/FREEDOM	_____	SELFISHNESS/JUDGING	_____
LOVE/HUMILITY	_____	BAD HABITS	_____
/KINDNESS EFFORT	_____	ANGER/PRIDE/INSINCERITY	_____

TOTAL CURRENT ASSETS =	[ ]	**TOTAL CURRENT LIABILITIES =**	[ ]
FIXED ASSETS		**LONG TERM LIABILITIES**	
BODY	_____	ADDICTIONS	_____
MIND	_____	UNFULFILLED DESIRES	_____
SOUL	_____	LOW SELF ESTEEM	_____
TOTAL FIXED ASSETS	_____	**TOTAL LONG TERM LIABILITIES**	_____
TOTAL ASSETS =	[ ]	**TOTAL LIABILITIES =**	[ ]
TOTAL CONSCIOUSNESS NET WORTH=	[ ]	(TOTAL ASSETS - TOTAL LIABILITIES)	

Max+/- score "10" per line   Signed/Date:

At the end of the exercise you will have your own score - your *Total Consciousness Net Worth*. If you like, give this a go every six months to track your progress.

Are You Ready to Flip The Switch?

FEELING GUILTY WHEN REPEATING UNHEALTHY HABITS?

✧ YOU FEEL   Disappointed and frustrated.

✧ YOU THINK   *I failed again. I may as well give up.*

✧ FLIP THE SWITCH   *I'm counting my blessings, not my failures – they're just small bumps in the road. I'll create small pockets of time to introduce good habits to give less time to my bad habits. If I catch myself thinking "I can't change", I will add the word 'yet' with a smile.*

OVERCOMING RESISTANCE TO HEALTHY LIVING

✧ YOU FEEL   Tired, miserable and unmotivated.

✧ YOU TELL YOURSELF *I can't be bothered to get up early to go to the gym and I don't have time to cook.*

✧ FLIP THE SWITCH   *Health isn't a luxury – it's my lifeline. I'm worth the effort. I feel genuinely better when I work out and eat well. Every Sunday, I'll plan a few exciting homemade meals – even just for three dinners a week. I'll also make a clear, achievable fitness plan and stick to it. Even if I start with fifteen minutes every day, I will start small and build solid foundations. And if my mind protests, I will tell it to MYOB!*

Change Tactics

How about tailoring your own positive affirmations for self-awareness, personal growth and healthy living? Remember to be fully conscious of the *prana* in each breath.

Add your words below:

I am inspired to commit to...

I am inspired to change my...

I am inspired to be kind to myself by...

You're in control of your destiny. Be kind and loving to yourself. Keep the faith. Listen to your dreams. Your actions will turn them into reality.

Before we get to the next page, do you fancy a few moments of meditation to chill out a bit?

Turn back to Secret #9 to remind yourself how to meditate.

If you are on audio, there's a bonus meditation.

PART SEVEN

INSPIRATION
MANIFESTATION & MOTIVATION

Turn Insights into Action

INSPIRATION
MANIFESTATION & MOTIVATION

In Part Seven, we talk about magic. The secret wisdom continues whispering in your ear - about inspiration, manifesting your destiny, laughing at failure, and much more. In Contemplation Corner, you can reflect on your attitude, your dream job and what inspires you. We then pause to listen to the inner voice speaking to us from inside. And the final motivation zone is more light-hearted...think superpowers, music and dreams!

> *"What you seek is seeking you."*
> Rumi, famous 13th century poet.

The Magic of Manifestation

Stay in tune with the flow of the moment. Feel the breath the life-force breathing *through* you. Gentle breath. Conscious breathing. In and out of the nostrils. No control, only awareness. Keep your attention in the centre of the chest; the heart chakra, the seat of the soul. When love guides us in everything we do, that's when the magic happens.

A person with absolute faith never plans or worries about tomorrow. For the rest of us, as our faith, mental fitness and humility grow, our energy field begins to align with what we truly seek.

Positive thoughts do much more than lift our mood - they literally light up the brain; triggering activity in neural pathways linked to happiness, clear thinking and deeper emotional connection.

Earlier I asked you to remember
four words...   *Be Great. Be Grateful.*

Now also add these four words to
your locker   *Think different. Become different.*

Transformation begins firstly in thoughts and then in action.

Be The Witness

When we step back and witness life being *done* through us, the miracles and manifestations come when we least expect. I've seen it happen first-hand.

Before my business was sold, like with most deals, a handful of sticking points remained which could make or break the deal. I was sitting on a bench in my suit eating a sandwich before a crunch meeting. At that time everyone in the City wore a suit. Out of nowhere, an Indian man, dressed casually, approached me. He told me, "*Good fortune is coming to you in the next few months.*" I smiled and thanked him. He walked away not approaching anyone else. It was a beautiful message from the Universe. A message of calm. Everything will work out just fine. *And* it did. All in the space of an unexpected, twenty-second encounter with a stranger. Any success that followed, felt less like achievement and more like grace from the Universe.

The Magic of Inspiration

The big dilemma...who can help unlock the wisdom already inside of you?

Only you can change your mind, your life and your attitude - but most of us still need a mentor or a guide along the way.

You've heard of the word *guru*. In Sanskrit, *Gu* means invisible, *Ru* means visible. The guru shows us how to manifest the wisdom that's hiding inside into full view. We all need inspiration. The question is who do we turn to for inspiration when we've hit a dead end or our dreams still seem out of reach?

- ☆ Who can give constructive feedback?
- ☆ Whose advice can we trust to help achieve our potential?
- ☆ Who offers honesty without ego or personal agenda?

Whoever you choose, be honest with yourself and the person in front of you. If we cling tight to our negatives and our ego, we can never grow.

I'm often asked for advice about business, finance, meditation and personal problems. For some reason since young, even strangers share their secrets with me. I've observed that most people fall into two distinct categories when seeking advice.

The High Achievers

Already well on the way to success - they're just seeking extra fine-tuning around strategy, goals or mindset.

High achievers really value the time of the mentor or adviser. They choose their mentor very carefully - not someone who simply agrees with them, but someone who has been up the mountain and come back down again.

I've noticed that the high achievers often take extensive notes, express gratitude and display zero ego. They are in tune with themselves, adapt suggestions quickly to their situation or articulate what's blocking their progress.

The high achievers come to pick your brains without pride and learn what they can from your knowledge and experience.

The In-Betweeners

We've all been here at one point in our life. Stuck, overwhelmed, overloaded - not knowing which way to turn. Sometimes we want change but aren't quite ready to act. That's completely human. The key is to recognise the difference between seeking a solution and seeking sympathy. Both have value, but only one moves us forward.

It's not that we don't want to change. We do, but fear, ego and self-doubt hold us hostage and at worst we risk self-sabotage. Deep down, if we remain stuck and lack confidence, we will be forever sitting in groundhog day. When we're ready to take ownership of our problems, the right guidance comes. If we stay too long in a place of indecision, we risk blocking our own path to happiness.

As someone who seeks smarter people than me for guidance, I'm always looking for the solution. In the role of adviser, I've discovered it's best to follow the simple rule, "One two, that'll do." Advise once, then again. After that, be the loving witness. It's hardest when it's someone you love.

There's a saying, which describes people who do not take responsibility, "I found myself in a ditch crying - I couldn't find my way out - but I dug the ditch myself." We have to be ready to *ditch* the ego.

Personal growth and self-awareness rest solely with us. We can't expect change if we're unwilling to change ourselves.

THE BIG SECRET TO ASKING

WHO TO ASK
Someone who has practical experience and knowledge who has the confidence to challenge you honestly.

WHAT TO ASK
Reading a menu ten times will not satisfy your hunger. Repeating your problems ten times won't make them go away. Ask for insight, not sympathy. Think. Feel. Stop, then act. If you try something

new, what's the best outcome you can visualise? Keep that thought. All will work out.

How to Listen
Drop the assumptions. Listen with a quiet mind. Have the attitude, "I know nothing."

How to Absorb Advice
Be the victor not the victim. Drop the facade. Don't be defensive. The Universe is on your side. Be open.

How to Proceed
Slow and steady. Take calm, deliberate steps. Change with mindful discipline. Start now.

The Magic of Calmness

It's surreal for me to revisit my silence experience - reliving moments of insight, calmness and emotions. Here are a few more diary entries centred around calmness. My biggest lesson? Stop giving myself a hard time.

* * * SILENCE DIARY EXTRACTS * * *

Day 45: My Meditation is Pitiful

"5.09am. Breath on the right."

[As part of my yogic practices I observe which side the breath flows from when I wake up. I've been taught it's more auspicious for the first exhale of the day to be from the right nostril on Tuesdays, Thursdays, Saturdays and Sundays. From the left nostril, on Mondays, Wednesdays and Fridays].

"Meditate until 7.39. Exercises next. It's rained all night and still going strong. Breakfast. Feeling just OK."

[I never wear a watch, but in silence, I decided to record when I woke up, the time I went to bed and how long I meditated.].

"I contemplate how pitiful my meditation practice really is. It should be full of love and gratitude. I've been given numerous techniques but honestly I cannot say I deserve them. It's inspiring to read about the lives of saints, many of whom experienced enormous difficulties. I can't help thinking that their greatness, their love for everyone and everything, makes me feel like an incomplete human being, devoid of spirituality.

I cry. Tears from deep within. Not emotional, more like a cleansing. I lie down. A message comes loud and clear from the voice inside. I know this voice is direct from the secret wisdom inside of me, as it's so strong and complete: *'David, don't do anything which deviates off the Path to Truth. You're on the right track.'*

If I weren't in silence I would be speechless!

The breath is calm. The mind is steady. This silence experience is becoming intense. Little did I know that on day 45, I am only 15% into the experience.

Thought of the Day: Leave everything behind."

* * *

Day 47: Stillness and Calmness

Thought of the Day: "Stillness and calmness are not enough. Only love will take me to the truth."

* * *

Day 70: Going with the ups and downs

"Feeling much more balanced now it's slightly cooler. Outside, the apple trees are growing - the blossoms have transformed into tiny apples, small, perfectly rounded and quietly taking shape. It's important to remember not to give myself a hard time when I'm feeling below par. The apple tree accepts the good and bad weather - so should I. I keep expecting more calmness and more progress. I hate the negative moments. I've become too used to expecting continuous days of uninterrupted bliss. I feel more in tune with the Universe. *God* isn't quite the right word. *IT* feels more accurate - formless, nameless, and beyond measure - yet limitless, all-encompassing, loving, and quietly nourishing. To believe is one thing. Experiencing is quite another. This phenomenon feels unfamiliar but comforting, rather than frightening.

Thought of the Day: Gratefulness makes us great. Great people think they are ordinary."

* * *

Day 83: Sitting it out when the going gets tough

"Awake for a while. 7.19-9.00am, meditation. Not deep.

Cloudy again. Focus today is on the pituitary gland."

[This is where I suggest you focus when meditating, just above the eyebrows, or in the centre of the chest].

"Meditate again, then walk. When I walk I am aware of *IT* breathing through me. Love and happiness in every step.

Temperature warms up to 24°C.

Feeling calm and balanced. When we are frustrated or unhappy in day-to-day life, we can immerse ourselves in distractions - watch a movie, social media, friends, or doing something unhealthy. None of these options are available in silence. It means I just have to sit and watch every thought and movement. The good, the bad and the ugly."

[I pause and describe in my diary a summary of my experience so far.]

"Each day is different…many experiences…inconsistent sleep patterns…crazy dreams…the internal world has become more important than the external world. Disconnection. Like I am being deep cleaned. No escaping my imperfections! Slowly being cooked. Can't run or hide. Conscious of *IT, The Invisible Hand* behind life.

It strikes me how much the world (parents, friends, family, peers) expects from us and how much we expect of the world. Both are recipes for dissatisfaction and unhappiness - the never-ending spiral of unfulfilled desires."

* * *

Day 91: The Inner Void

"Wake about 5.30. Drifted back to sleep. Dreamt I was buying a cool pair of shoes and then jumped into a new Aston Martin, revving up outside."

[I don't own one, by the way!]

"Get up 7.32. Zero tension in me. Am thinking of the ultimate state of mind. Total cessation. A neutral mind. Can we mortals reach that state? This silence experience shows me that every meditative and mindful moment leads to profound inner peace when we manifest our loving, non-reactive, non-judgemental, peaceful and happy nature.

No rush today. Let everything unfold. Feels great. *IT* is doing. *I AM BEING*. Meditate 8.15-10.07. Lawnmower noisy outside. No problem. It will pass. Amazing meditation. Like meditating in an inner void; a space without walls. Nothingness. No movement. Still breath. Just silence. If thoughts come, they don't enter the inner void of peace. Unfamiliar. Beautiful. The silent chamber is impenetrable."

* * *

Insights from Silence

I hope these diary entries inspire you to sit quietly with yourself, a few minutes a day, to listen to the silence inside. I'm not sharing my experiences to show any achievement - you'll see I had dark moments, all the more intense being alone.

We all wrestle with self-doubt, unhappiness and restlessness. In silence, I found inspiration and answers I didn't think I needed - and you will too. Maybe not on day one! If you stay open and just watch, something shifts - the voice of inner wisdom becomes clearer. And the reminder that just as you are, is *already* ENOUGH.

Calmness isn't the absence of thought, it's the presence of trust.

Your Turn

Feeling inspired? Ready to manifest the *real you*?

> What pledge are you going to make to increase your calmness?
> Note down your goals...
> Remind yourself of your amazing qualities...
> Write down your rescue plan if you fall off track...

SECRET #43

HOW TO BE INSPIRED
by turning ideas into action

The secret wisdom whispers in your ear

An ounce of practice is worth more than a ton of theories
An ounce of love is worth more than a ton of gold
An ounce of humility is worth more than a ton of snobbery

An ounce of happiness is worth more than a ton of misery
An ounce of kindness is worth more than a ton of selfishness
An ounce of clarity is worth more than a ton of confusion

An ounce of common sense is worth more than a ton of gobbledygook
An ounce of meditation is worth more than a ton of restlessness
An ounce of faith is worth more than a ton of doubts

An ounce of success is worth more than a ton of failure
An ounce of self-confidence is worth more than a ton of fear
An ounce of effort is worth more than a ton of laziness
An ounce of self-analysis is worth more than a ton of self-criticism
An ounce of dignity is worth more than a ton of pomposity

Who wants to be inspired?

MINDFUL THOUGHTS ON BEING INSPIRED

"In theory, theory and practice are the same. In practice, they are not." Attributed to Albert Einstein.

It's worth contemplating the inner battle that many of us face daily...

Love, common sense, humility, happiness, kindness, clarity, faith, success, self-confidence, effort and dignity;

versus...

Hate, snobbery, arrogance, misery, selfishness, confusion, restlessness, doubts, failure, fear, laziness and pomposity.

With effort, there can be only one winner and one inner friend worth keeping.

SECRET #44

HOW TO UNLEASH YOUR UNLIMITED POTENTIAL
with courage, belief and confidence

The secret wisdom whispers in your ear

Nearly Impossible is Definitely Possible!

To reach our goals we need a plan...
...we need to know how
THEN
...we need to know why

Potential and ability are only useful...
...when we are prepared to do what it takes
...when we know how to concentrate on the goal
...when we demonstrate wisdom and accumulate useful knowledge

Knowing who to ask is a skill
Knowing who to trust is a must
Knowing who to work with is mastery

Like it or not, today's reality is the result of your past efforts...
...today's reality is the proof of your past
...the stepping stone to your future

To make the decision to be successful is the first step

To make the decision not to repeat past mistakes is the second
step

...to use your time valuably is the third step

Making no decision, often leads to helplessness and despair
What's the best way ahead?

Have courage and faith, my friend!

If you don't know something, then find someone that does
If you don't know which career to pursue, then start a job
which matches your passion
If you don't know how to control the mind, then meditate

Who wants to unleash their unlimited potential?

MINDFUL THOUGHTS ON UNLEASHING YOUR UNLIMITED POTENTIAL

To reach your unlimited potential you have to believe YOU
CAN from the core of your being. Make your beliefs count.
Make them second nature, so that success has no choice but to
come.

Be charismatic. A bit of schmooze never hurt anyone. Quit
giving yourself a tough time if you fail an exam, lose a job or
lose your temper now and again. But sometimes you have to be
honest to be kind to yourself. You have to face up to what *you
are doing* and *not doing, and* if you are experiencing a boring,
difficult and tiresome life.

Sit quietly for five minutes. Smile and visualise yourself as an invincible warrior instead of a compulsive worrier. I mean it. Try it!

Now sit for ten minutes. Think of all your amazing qualities. Afterwards write down three negative traits that are giving you trouble. Burn the piece of paper. Watch it go up in smoke, but don't burn the house down.

Switching your mindset isn't about thinking harder, it's about thinking clearly. Shift into turbo mode with total conviction to reach your highest goals and noble desires.

Are you celebrating life?
If not
START TODAY

SECRET #45

HOW TO CREATE A ROUTINE THAT BRINGS SUCCESS
by turning theory into practice

The secret wisdom whispers in your ear

A strict life is a boring life
A regimented life is a tiresome life
A humdrum life is a dreary life
A passionate life is an exhausting life

How do we balance passion with compassion?
How do we balance work with play, discipline with fun,
success with less stress?

Increasing our strengths brings worthwhile discipline
Repeating our weaknesses destroys worthwhile discipline
Increasing our strengths unlocks the door to success
Repeating our weaknesses unlocks the door to failure
Increasing our good habits is the key to contentment and
happiness
Repeating our unhealthy habits is the key to restlessness and
unhappiness

Discipline with love rewards our efforts
Disciplining the mind is possible with daily meditation

Start today with a plan
Start by introducing one new, positive habit every Monday

Continue weekly

Spending valuable time on new, positive habits automatically crowds out our negative habits

Continue

If you fall, get up and go again

Fools waste time

Fools squander every breath daydreaming about a better tomorrow

Don't wait 'til tomorrow

Do it now

Banish excuses

BECAUSE

Only you suffer the consequences

Live in the *now*

Live with a *smile*

Live with the power of vitality, vibrancy and vibration

Who wants to create a routine that brings success?

❧

MINDFUL THOUGHTS ON CREATING A ROUTINE THAT BRINGS SUCCESS

Self-discipline is essential to channel your inner drive to ensure you achieve the success you deserve.

Make smiling and laughter part of your *hourly* routine.

It's 100% in your power to do what is good for you and to stop what is bad for you.

Stop moaning. Start doing. Don't be a miserable git! That's your cue to laugh not sulk.

"A day without laughter is a wasted day." Charlie Chaplin

The quickest way to find a quick fix is to fix your attitude

CONTEMPLATION CORNER

☆ Inspiration ☆ Sticking to a Routine ☆
Meeting our Potential ☆

Feeling positive today? Here's an inspirational quote from Audrey Hepburn, the great Hollywood actress and philanthropist who dedicated her life to children's rights.

Her motto was: "Nothing is impossible. The word itself says *I'm possible*!"

Sometimes we have to look to previous role models to inspire our own wisdom.

WHO INSPIRES YOU THE MOST? WHY?

HOW CAN YOU USE YOUR UNIQUE SPECIAL QUALITIES TO INSPIRE AND
SERVE THE WORLD EVEN MORE?

LIST THREE EFFECTIVE CHANGES TO YOUR ROUTINE YOU ARE
PREPARED TO MAKE TO BRING MORE DISCIPLINE AND FUN:

SECRET #46

HOW TO MANIFEST YOUR DESTINY
just do it!

The secret wisdom whispers in your ear

This life brings choices
...ideas
...temptation

This life brings distraction
...distress
...happiness

This life remains empty if we live like robots

The empty beach patiently awaits your gentle footprints to magically signpost the way ahead
The empty ocean calmly awaits you as you swim towards the rainbow on the horizon

Have courage...
...to rise above mediocrity
...to rise *above* your potential
Have courage to manifest and follow your destiny...
...to be free to choose what *you* want to do and not what others *expect* you to do
...to be free to choose where you live and how you spend your day
...to be free to choose freedom instead of misery

To fulfil your destiny, you have to be free from your negatives
Free from the negatives of others
Free from hypocrisy and greed...
From jealousy and anger
From despair and boredom
Free to express yourself without hurting others

Are you living a free-flowing life full of *joie de vivre*?
or
a barren life devoid of humour?

Stuck in an uninspiring routine?
Same faces on the bus or on the train?
Same packed lunch?
Same traffic on the way home?
Same problems?

Bored but pretending to be content?
Unhappy but wearing the fake mask of happiness?
What do you choose?
If you're unhappy, deep down you know what to do!

Who wants to manifest their destiny?

MINDFUL THOUGHTS ON
HOW TO MANIFEST YOUR DESTINY

Analyse your daily life.

Create a plan of change and slowly execute step by step.

Look four steps ahead and take one step forward calmly.

Change is a choice. What's your choice?

Just Do It!

ASK YOURSELF: *Who do I need to become to create the outcome I desire?*

Feel like a quick mind check?
Go Back to Pages 92 and 93.
Has your score improved?

SECRET #47

HOW TO LAND YOUR DREAM JOB
you actually love

The secret wisdom whispers in your ear

Dream jobs exist but...

...are you dreaming or doing?

Dreamers dream...

...and dream again - over and over again

Time steals our ambition and youth...

...until it's too late

Doers become movers and shakers

Doers awaken success while others just dream

Doers make their dreams materialise

Have faith and courage, my friend

Dream jobs manifest with determination, confidence and humility

Dream jobs manifest when we change our approach

We all want our dream job but what's so interesting and special about *us* to land that job?

What's so extraordinary about you?

If you want your dream job, you need to increase your chances by making new connections daily...

...you need to change your mindset daily

...you need to improve your attitude daily

...you need to enhance your skillset daily

If you want your dream job, how can you improve yourself to land that job?

As part of adding value to yourself...

Banish all negatives and super-boost your positives

Keep a healthy distance from negative news and negative views

A drop of negativity is like a drop of poison...

...it spoils everything...

My friend, to dream is positive

But now is the time to live the *dream* and leave behind the *nightmare*

The secret to landing your dream job is hidden inside of you

The secret wisdom never lies

Who is ready to land their dream job?

MINDFUL THOUGHTS ON LANDING YOUR DREAM JOB

Today is the result of the past and today will determine your future.

How you see yourself and how others see you is the key to unlocking your dream job. A bubbling personality with a dynamic *can do* attitude is a must in an interview.

The great psychologist Robert Rosenthal discovered the Pygmalion Effect in 1968.

He selected children from one class at a school for a social experiment. The parents and teachers were told that the "chosen" children had the highest potential. None of them knew that the kids had been selected randomly, regardless of ability. These children, without their knowledge, were reinforced with positive encouragement only because the parents and teachers now believed they were special. A year later *all* of them were ahead of their contemporaries.

Rosenthal concluded "that what one person expects of another can come to serve as a self-fulfilling prophecy."

The secret wisdom has every confidence in you. You can do it!

Find a way to get to the highest decision-maker to let them know you exist.

"Believe you can and you are halfway there." Theodore Roosevelt, 26th US President.

MOMENTUM MAKER

What does your next job look like? Write a description. List the skills you need to carry out your dream role. Now circle one skill each week to improve upon.

Create a small version of your dream job now.

Want to be a writer? Start a blog.

Thinking of healthcare? Volunteer one evening per week at a local charity in your sector of interest.

Want to be CEO? Come up with an idea and launch a side project.

Fancy being a tour guide? Learn the history of a city and offer a free guided walk.

Want to be an accountant? Study numbers and betting.

Oh sorry, that's a turf accountant.

When I'm not feeling 100%, the main question that whizzes around in my head is "What am I doing with my life?"

After meditation, the whirring slows down.

What's your big question today?

What's your big answer today?

SECRET #48

HOW TO LAUGH AT FAILURE
and bounce back

The secret wisdom whispers in your ear

Is failure a blessing or a curse?
Failure can be a blessing that gives us the opportunity to
reflect

Failure is a way to correct ourselves
...to improve ourselves
...a way to catalyse change that *changes* us - not change for its
own sake
Failure is a way to revitalise our lives
...to inspire us to do something that matters
Failure is a small diversion on our path to success

What's important in life to us *really*?
Take a glass of fresh juice
Put your feet up for a few minutes
Conscious breathing
Close your eyes for a few moments
Take a chill pill
Metaphorically of course!

Contemplate for a moment these words
We work hard to study
to improve ourselves

to achieve more

The short-term result may or may not go to plan

When we do our best, the Universe will do the rest

Every sincere effort brings personal growth

When we don't do our best, why should we expect a positive result?

Life matters much more than passing or failing...

Life is greater than our desires

Life is greater than our discontented minds

We strive for recognition, for importance, for power

We strive for success, too often to impress

THE BIG SECRET is to strive for stillness...

...to attain contentment

...to brush off our failures with a smile

Life is the greatest teacher

Our best isn't always enough

Persevere

Smile

The dust of the past is past

THE BIG SECRET is to smile and laugh when you face adversity and temporary failure

AND

To accept failure as part of deferred success

Who is ready to laugh at failure?

MINDFUL THOUGHTS ON LAUGHING AT FAILURE

A JOKE ABOUT FAILURE

I went to my therapist. The therapist told me my problems are all solvable, but I keep blaming everyone else without taking responsibility. I replied, "I get that from my parents!"

Failure is just a stepping stone to success.

Avoid people with ego and pride - the ones who hide their failures and project fake perfection.

"Success is not final; failure is not fatal. It is the courage to continue that counts." Winston Churchill.

FAILURE CELEBRATION

Pour a glass of your favourite drink. Press the *Zen Button. Be the Witness. So What!*

FLIP THE SWITCH

Celebrate your courage - not for succeeding, but for having a go. Remember, *the professionals* told me my business would fail. They were wrong.

Reframe failure as a necessary part of growth. Learn from it. Let it teach you.

Break free from disappointment. Something better will come.

SECRET #49

HOW TO LEAD A LIFE OF TRANQUILLITY
without being a boring ass

The secret wisdom whispers in your ear

Steady Mind, Steady Life
Greedy Mind, Greedy Life
Steady Money, Steady Life

Greedy Desires, Greedy Life
Greedy & Needy, Never Happy

Happy Life, Calm Life
Calm Life, Fulfilling Life
Steady Relationship, Loving Life

Without Fulfilment, Peace Remains Out of Reach.
Without Peace, Troubles Never Cease
The Secret of Living a Life of Tranquillity?
Just Be
Sounds schmaltzy - but it's true

Stress is a consequence of life's daily struggles
Stress can be obliterated by meditation
Stress works against our true nature...
...to be calm
...to be relaxed

Who's bored of being stressed?

Who's bored of never sleeping, through hurry and worry?
Who's bored and unfulfilled?

With meditation...
Calmness arrives in the midst of the chaos
Calmness arrives in the nick of time
Like a wise friend whispering
"Let it all go"
Calmness comes with crystal-clarity

Calmness and Stillness
Stillness and Peace
Peace and Bliss
Bliss and Tranquillity

Tranquillity blesses us with self-assurance
with wisdom
with confidence
with a smile

Be warned
To follow the path of peace needs courage
To walk away from the noise
To pause...
...when the world is shouting "go!"

That's bravery
To go against the norm

So, who really wants to lead a life of tranquillity?

MINDFUL THOUGHTS ON TRANQUILLITY

If tranquillity were a holiday destination, where would it be? A sun-kissed beach in Bali? A mystical forest? A mountain sunrise?

Why dream it when you can create it?

Set up a calmness corner in your home - your private sanctuary of peace. Comfy chair. Your favourite book. A leafy plant. And yes, a *snack attack* drawer full of goodies. Bare feet. Be still in the flow of the moment. Feel the life-force in each breath.

ARE YOU FOLLOWING THIS
ANCIENT PEARL OF WISDOM?

*"Never Delay Something Good until Tomorrow.
Always Delay What is Bad for You Indefinitely."*

SECRET #50

HOW TO MAKE YOUR DREAMS A REALITY
without falling asleep

The secret wisdom whispers in your ear

The end is near
The end of the book
The end of our dreams
The beginning of realisation

To dream is imagination
To achieve is reality

You dream about success...
...about your ideal partner
...about a better life
...about making more money

You dream and dream and, in a moment, life is over
My beautiful friend, dreaming is wonderful
Dreaming motivates you...inspires you....helps you to succeed

When the dreaming ends, you *must* wake up
Then, and only then, does realisation begin
Realisation is the key to make your dreams a reality...
...to unleash your strengths and diminish your weaknesses
To kick-start your life

What must you realise to achieve your goals?

How can you activate the dormant power inside?
What must you change to realise your goals?

The present moment always speaks the naked truth
Are you over-dreaming and under-achieving?
OR
Are you already over-achieving, too busy to dream?

The present moment is the creative millisecond that will
determine your future
The present moment is the sum of your past

NOW is the MOMENT to DO
To CHANGE
To IMPROVE
To acquire NEW SKILLS

To achieve you need to...
DOUBLE your effort
TRIPLE your focus
QUADRUPLE your wisdom
QUINTUPLE your courage
INFINITELY multiply your common sense

Enjoy your journey to unlimited success

Do you want to make your dreams into your reality?

MINDFUL THOUGHTS ON
MAKING YOUR DREAMS A REALITY

The time for dreaming has ended. The time for doing is now.
Dreamers DREAM. Doers DO. Which are you?

Steady Mind = *Balanced Life*
Greedy Mind = *Greedy Life*
Laughing Mind = *Joyful Life*

CONTEMPLATION CORNER

☆ Manifesting our Destiny ☆ Failure ☆ Making our Dreams a Reality ☆ Tranquillity ☆

Failure is just a bump in the road. Keep going. Slow and steady wins the race.

IS DESTINY IN OUR HANDS OR PRE-DETERMINED?

Maybe both. The more we align with our true nature, through healthy living, meditation and conscious mindfulness, the more we clearly see the path ahead and the *more* we know what to do. How to handle difficulties. How to live more fully. Either way, the one truth that sets us free is, *we must take responsibility.*

ACTION WITH PURPOSE IS THE FOUNDATION TO SUCCESS.

Now ask yourself once again, am I dreamy, a dreamer, or a doer?

DO YOU HAVE A RECURRING DREAM? WHAT'S IT TRYING TO TELL YOU?

Are you ready to make your dreams a reality to fulfil your potential?

PAUSE AND REFLECT

WHAT'S MY DREAM JOB?

WHICH BELIEFS HELP ME AND WHICH ONES HOLD ME BACK?

WHAT AM I PREPARED TO DO TO LIVE A LIFE LESS CHAOTIC THAN NOW?

REFLECTIONS

The Magic Pill

Everyone is looking for instant success and gratification. After all, we live in a world of magic pills or injections that *promise* to help us lose weight, stop our headaches, help us sleep, or to relieve our anxiety. The marketing message is clear - take more pills and carry on!

The Truth About The Quick Fix

Of course, I really wish I could offer you one magic pill to manifest your dreams of success in less than a second. In fact, I bet a queue would form around the corner, even if it cost £250,000 per pill.

The great news is that the magic pill you seek is already inside of you. It costs nothing. It's the accumulation of your efforts, your skills, your personality and your attitude. If you persevere, you'll reach *saturation* point - the invisible atom point. That moment when all your efforts flow together - unfolding into something greater than you can ever imagine.

As you've reached the end of the book, you've already decided to make the effort to live a fulfilling life. The hardest part is to keep balance, keep perspective and keep your personal life on an even keel.

Listening to your Inner Voice

The secret wisdom is *always* whispering in your ear.

Softly, patiently, faithfully - with love.

That inner voice of truth. Guiding and nurturing you.

The secret wisdom is your best guide. Always helping you.

This special inner wisdom so often drowned out by this noisy world of thoughts and drama.

Just stop. Listen. Feel. Think.

To know your truth and to be in your truth is the royal path to meaningful success.

To find the way to JUST BE.

The Power of Meditation

Just a short daily practice, at the height of my career, transformed my life.

Are you now convinced it can help you too?

Meditation reveals your inner truth and clarity

Your deep consciousness. Your sacred silence. Always waiting for you.

Your truth may lead you to change course.

Letting go of familiarity. Embracing possibilities. Embracing the new.

Choose Your Path

You have the power to choose your unique path to wisdom, freedom and contentment...

...the power to find meaningful success.

...the power to change yourself and to attract what you want in your life.

Mindset is Everything

Saints and sages since time immemorial have given us the gift of meditation.

Meditation is beyond any religion. It's for all of us regardless of our beliefs.

Like it or not - if you do nothing, you get nothing.

If you complain that nobody helps, you will remain stuck in a rut.

If you have a negative attitude that life is tough, then it will be tough.

If you have a positive attitude, it's inevitable - *you must and will* achieve your goals.

If you ask for help, help comes.

Be a triumphant victor in life. Be grateful for your blessings. Light the fire within. Be refreshed.

Walk your path with confidence. Trust in your ability to succeed.

Redefining Success

Each of us has our own idea of success. Regardless of what we want to achieve, we need the same core ingredients - skill, motivation and drive, to go beyond what society tells us we need or want.

Average effort = Average results.

Extra effort   = Excellent results

Nobody ever achieved anything by giving up.

Gratitude, humility and contentment are the real rewards of success.

If you want success enough... it's all yours!

MOTIVATION ZONE

At the start of the book, I asked you to say out loud five big questions:

☆ What's the point of dreaming if my dreams do not become my reality?
☆ What's the point of working, day in day out, when freedom feels so far away?
☆ What's the point of measuring my career success, but never measuring my happiness?
☆ What's the point of enduring constant stress and unhappiness just to exist?
☆ What's the point of following a path that does not make me feel truly, deeply happy?

If you read aloud these questions now, what is your reaction? The same as before or different? How is it different? Have your priorities changed? Are you ready to rock 'n' roll?

I hope so. A gentle reminder: As we think so we are. As we feel so we are. As we love so we are.

In the quietest moments, truth reveals itself to us. To inspire and manifest - perhaps you now see the benefits to sit and listen to the secret wisdom inside. To be calmer, maybe you now see the benefits of meditation and conscious mindfulness.

Do you agree that silence brings the answers that a busy mind will never see? My hope is you are brimming with confidence with extra tools to navigate life! How are you feeling? Ready to jump out of the ditch?

Ok hang on! We're getting a bit serious. Here's a quiz. Just for fun.

If your motivation had a catch phrase what would it be?
☆ Nap now, conquer later.
☆ Protein shake first, empire building, second.
☆ Procrastinate like a visionary, Execute like a ninja.
☆ Create your own catch phrase here...

If Your Dream Were a Movie, What Would It Be?

◈ La La Land — Dancing through delusion and still manifesting magic

◈ The Matrix — You took the red pill, now what?

◈ Honey, I Shrunk the Kids — You messed up. You can't undo it. Tell everyone the neighbour's dog ate your masterplan.

Add your dream movie here...

If Your Mind Had a Soundtrack What Would It Be?

◈ Don't Stop Me Now — Your brain after five cups of coffee and it's only 11am.

◈ I'm Still Standing — When survival mode kicks in and it's only Monday!

◈ Under Pressure — Winging it with a smile when underneath you don't have a clue.

Add your dream soundtrack here...

If You Could Choose a Superpower What Would It Be?

◈ Alchemy — Transform panic into power in one short breath

✧ TIME TRAVEL	Bend time so your holiday never ends
✧ TELEPATHY	One thought and the world finally loves and understands you. No more explaining yourself to people who never listened to you in the first place!

Add your superpower here...

Momentum Maker

Don't worry if things don't go to plan.

✧ TRY THIS	Track your negatives for a day and practise reframing them. Pause, reflect, don't judge.
✧ YOU FEEL	Worried that things aren't going to plan
✧ YOU THINK	*I'm constantly making the wrong decisions*
✧ FLIP THE SWITCH	*I'm still learning. Next time I'll try a different approach. I'll not react. I'll tune into my inner coach, not my inner critic.*
✧ AFFIRMATION	*I choose thoughts that empower me and to ignore thoughts and people who weaken me.*
✧ BE EXTRAORDINARY!	How about harnessing your superpowers? Determination, courage, cheerfulness and common sense will surely catapult you towards your goals.
✧ BE ENTHUSIASTIC!	Your enthusiasm will create a wave of positive people who want to be around you and support your vision. Maximising the abilities you have already is the way to even more success.

✧ Be Positive!   Remember your mini-successes and not your mini-failures.

Nobody wants to be around a person who thinks their life is tougher than anyone else's.

✧ Be Real!   It's unlikely that you're going to outrun Usain Bolt, even now he has retired, no matter how focussed your visualisation techniques. But what would happen if you increased your talents by just 1% each week? Diminish your negatives by grabbing your mind.

✧ Be Dynamic!   No excuses. Tap into your dynamic powers. You're already super-smart. Recognise your skills. When you feel like quitting, try and try again, but don't bang your head against a brick wall. You *will* find another way. And sometimes you may need to change course. So what!

✧ Be Authentic!   Guess what. You are as you are, regardless of who you want to be! Embrace your strengths, manifest your passion and create your own unique way to succeed.

✧ Be Courageous!   Your inner strength and courage can definitely turn adversity into your personal driver for success. You don't need to prove anything to anyone else. Define what *happy, meaningful success* looks like for you. Pursue at your own pace - keeping your integrity and joy intact.

Thought of The Day

You are not your thoughts. You have the power to change them.

If your mind had a mute button which thought would you shut out the most?

Choose the tools you want to incorporate into your daily routine. See what works for you. Find your own pace - your way.

INSPIRATION CORNER

Breaking news! The Secret Wisdom is You. Trust. Act. Shine.

The best answers to your own questions are already within you.

Have the courage to follow your beliefs.

Here are three heroes of mine, who inspire me daily.

ALBERT EINSTEIN

"There are only two ways to live your life. One is as though nothing is a miracle. The other is as though everything is a miracle."

VIKTOR FRANKL

"Bear witness to the uniquely human potential at its best, which is to transform a personal tragedy into a triumph, to turn one's predicament into a human achievement."

BRUCE LEE

"Success is when preparation meets opportunity."

FINAL REFLECTIONS

Are you ready to be successful? Any last thoughts? What do you love about your life?

What are you going to change about your life starting NOW?

How about picking up this book up in one year's time to compare your answers?

Be Great. Be Grateful. Think Different. Become Different.

Happy, meaningful success is guaranteed. You really have got this! I'm excited for you.

THE END

🎧 ENJOY THE FREE AUDIO!

Legal Blurb

As you will appreciate, the optional, complimentary audio is offered in good faith to enhance your reading experience. Free access is available only for 'new' book or 'new' e-book purchases. A quick sign-up is required to help keep the content secure. The audio is limited to one single ISP address, delivered via a specialist third-party audiobook platform.

As you will understand, neither the author nor the publisher can accept responsibility for technical issues, changes in availability, or any future access limitations. As usual, please use your discretion when accessing online content and ensure your device has appropriate security settings in place.

Separately, the audiobook will be available on its own as a paid version on leading audiobook platforms. To enhance the listening experience, the audiobook contains a few minor differences from the paperback and e-book editions.

Enjoy listening!

AFTERWORD

Time and tide wait for nobody.

The hourglass of life quietly runs down. Time slips away, often unnoticed, until it's too late. To live a complete life with meaning, success and contentment, we have to start now.

Each of us carries within us the seed of something greater. The potential to evolve spiritually and serve the world through our daily actions. Whatever we did yesterday we cannot change - but every new day offers the opportunity to go beyond our limitations, to become better, kinder and more loving, both at home and at work.

The Big Secret of How is a powerful and timely guide and companion - a book for all moments. It offers encouragement, clarity and calm for anyone seeking practical inspiration.

I have known David for nearly 30 years. I have witnessed his life close-up. His relentless work ethic, his struggles with burnout, stress and personal problems and his unwavering commitment to maintain his spiritual practice. His determination to work with intensity and succeed in his career, while always making time to meditate is living proof that no matter the challenges, it is possible to reflect, be mindful, meditate and succeed.

David's rare blend of expertise in business success, meditation, yoga and healthy living, turns profound insights into actionable tips. Whether the reader is seeking mental clarity, striving for professional advancement, or simply wanting to nurture their well-being and cultivate more calmness, the book covers it all in a way that feels both empowering and deeply relevant.

Years ago, I described David as being like a coconut - soft on the inside and tough on the outside. Direct and straightforward, but caring and sincere. Above all he has faith. Over the years the outside has softened. His love, his faith, his humour and sincerity shine through in this book.

I am really happy that he is sharing not only his story, but also his inner life - the doubts, the breakthroughs and his experiences in silence - all giving the reader insights, tools and encouragement to take the next step.

Human life is a rare gift. Use it wisely. May this book be a catalyst and a trusted companion on your path to *happy, meaningful success.*

"Guriji," Paramahamsa Prajnanananda Giri. Head of Kriya Yoga International.

DEDICATION

Huge appreciation and love to my many friends, readers and supporters, including - Karl French my editor and agent; Kirsty, Nadia, Sharon, Jean, Gill and Tony; *and* to Christine, who lovingly facilitated my silence challenge. Finally, to Guruji - the epitome of wisdom, love and laughter in action.

ABOUT THE FRONT COVER

The front cover designed by the author, features the Zen Buddhist symbol *ensō*, meaning "circle" in Japanese. Traditionally drawn in a single, unbroken brushstroke - clockwise or anti-clockwise. The *ensō*, was chosen to express the book's underlying ideas of dynamic energy, openness, inner awareness and the beauty of imperfection. The unclosed circle leaves space for change and fresh beginnings.

THE LOTUS FLOWER

Symbolism is a beautiful way to convey our love, our message and feelings towards the world.

The theme of using lotus leaves throughout the book represents the beauty of the lotus leaf that sits above the water unaffected above the water and the ground below, but rooted into the ground. Even when it rains the water and dirt trickles away. The message is to be in the world but to realise we are not of the world and to go beyond body consciousness and towards consciousness of the Soul.

ABOUT THE AUTHOR

David Green is a former bond trader and entrepreneur. He founded a niche business at 23 and built it from scratch to sale. He is an experienced practitioner of meditation and Kriya Yoga, having studied for nearly three decades under two masters from India. Following a 300-day silent retreat, he gave the World's first TEDx talk delivered entirely in silence.

Thirty years ago, at the height of his career, he began daily meditation and adopted a vegan lifestyle.

David advises individuals and organisations on how to integrate business acumen, meditation and spiritual wisdom into their decision-making, leadership approach, careers and personal lives.

His first book, *The Invisible Hand: Business, Success & Spirituality*, was published in 2013. He has also written on meditation, wellbeing and leadership for *The Huffington Post*, and spoken at various business forums, Soho House and other venues.

David is a Londoner who lives in Guernsey. He supports educational charities in India and South Africa, including Hand in Hand's Balashram school in Odisha and the Bhongolethu Foundation near Cape Town.

To connect, visit www.davidgreen.uk

ACKNOWLEDGEMENTS

Before we finish, a quick note. A few short quotations from external sources appear throughout this book. These are used under fair dealing and fair use guidelines - supporting education, commentary, and transformation.

I've included them to add depth and context. Every effort has been made to credit original sources. Of course, all rights remain with the original copyright holders.

NOTES TO ACKNOWLEDGEMENTS IN CHRONOLOGICAL ORDER

HOW TO USE THIS BOOK

Aristotle: Paraphrased from Aristotle's Metaphysics Book VIII

PART ONE

Journal of Psychosomatic Research: *The Grossarth–Maticek et al. study: Vol. 75, Issue 5, 2013.*

Santiago Ramón y Cajal: *Advice for a Young Investigator* (1897), translated Neely Swanson (MIT Press 1999).

'20% genes, 30% conditioning and 50% conscious effort' - Yogic teachings from Baba Hariharananda, Kriya Yoga master

Leonardo da Vinci: Often attributed; wording not found in surviving manuscripts.

Direct Line Insurance: Press release, UK (March 2025): 5,500 mobile phones dropped into toilets daily (~ 2 million annually).

Thucydides: *History of the Peloponnesian War*, Book II, 43

Tallulah Bankhead:- *Tallulah, My Autobiography* (New York: Harper & Brothers, 1952).

Guru Nanak: Guru Granth Sahib p.1089

Thich Nhat Hanh: Theme of his teachings, including *Fear: Essential Wisdom for Getting Through the Storm* (Parallax Press, 2012).

PART TWO

Microsoft Canada: *Attention Spans, Consumer Insights* (Spring 2015); figure originates from "Statistic Brain."

David Green: *The Invisible Hand: Business, Success & Spirituality*, (Masters & Son Limited 2013).

Gandhi learning Kriya Yoga: *Autobiography of a Yogi* (New York: Philosophical Library, 1946)

Mother Teresa learning Kriya Yoga: Relayed to me by Baba Hariharananda. (Personal testimony).

Prana: *Atharva Veda, Book 11, Hymn 4 ("Prāṇa Sūkta")* et al., c. 1200-1000 BCE (early Vedic period).

Sage Vasistha: *Yoga Vasista* Nirvāṇa, Part 1, ch. 38, vv. 31-36, translated Swami Venkatesananda.

Alexander Pope: *An Essay on Man*, Epistle II, ll. 1-2 (1733-1734).

National Science Foundation: often attributed; no primary source found.

Steve Jobs and Autobiography of a Yogi: *Steve Jobs*, Walter Isaacson, 2011.

Émile Coué: *Self-Mastery Through Conscious Autosuggestion* (1922).

PART THREE

Audaces fortuna juvat: Virgil - *Aeneid*, Book 10, l. 284.

Carpe Diem: Horace - *Odes* 1.11.8.

Henry David Thoreau: *Faith in a Seed* (Island Press/Shearwater Books, 1993); written 1850s.

Leonard Cohen: "Anthem," *The Future* (Columbia Records, 1992).

Snoopy (Charles M. Schulz): Often attributed; original comic strip source not found.

Carl Rogers: Paraphrase from *On Becoming a Person* (Houghton Mifflin, 1961);

Scientific benefits of nasal breathing and nitric oxide: Lundberg, J.O. et al. (2008), *Nitric oxide and the paranasal sinuses*, *The Anatomical Record* 291(11):1479-1484 et al.

PART FOUR

Baba: Baba Hariharananda, Kriya Yoga master

Britta K. Hölzel et al. : Harvard/MGH Mindfulness MRI study, *Psychiatry Research: Neuroimaging* 191(1), 2011.

Thucydides: *Thucydides, History of the Peloponnesian War*, Book II, 43.4. (Pericles' Funeral Oration, paraphrase).

Mahatma Gandhi: "Seven Social Sins," first published in *Young India*, 1925:

Martin Luther King Jr. : Convocation address, Oberlin College, Ohio, 22 Oct 1964.

Brené Brown: "I am not here to be right. I am here to get it right." (*Dare to Lead*, 2018).

Ramakrishna Paramahamsa (1836-1886): Revered Indian saint and teacher.

PART FIVE

1 in 4 people in England experience mental health issues: *The Big Mental Health Report* (Mind, 2024).

1 in 7 adults in the UK are prescribed antidepressants: NHS Business Services Authority Digital (2024).

Helen Keller: *We Bereaved, 1933.*

Alexander Pope: *An Essay on Man, Epistle II, 1733-34.*

Epictetus (c. 55-135 AD): *Fragments*, no. 25, Stobaeus' *Anthology* (5th century)

William Bruce Cameron: *Informal Sociology: A Casual Introduction to Sociological Thinking* (Random House, 1963). Quote widely attributed to Albert Einstein.

Socrates (469-399 BC): As quoted in Diogenes Laërtius, *Lives of Eminent Philosophers* (3rd century AD).

PART SIX

Jim Rohn: *7 Strategies for Wealth and Happiness* (Bantam Books, 1985).

Eleanor Roosevelt: *This Is My Story* (Harper & Brothers, 1935).

Oracle Corporation: *Happiness Report* (2022). Global survey conducted with research partner Savanta.

Food and Agriculture Organization of the United Nations (FAO): *Livestock's Long Shadow: Environmental Issues and Options* (FAO, 2006).

Public Library of Science (PLOS): Umbrella review of 23 years of peer-reviewed studies on vegan and vegetarian health outcomes. *PLOS ONE* (2023).

Cleveland Clinic - "Chickpeas: Health Benefits, Nutrients, Preparation." *Cleveland Clinic Health Library* (2022).

Mood, A. et al.: "Numbers of Fish and Other Animals Killed for Food Every Year." *Animal Welfare* (Cambridge University Press, 2023).

Jeremy Bentham: *An Introduction to the Principles of Morals and Legislation* (1789), ch. XVII, s.1, fn:

Hippocrates: Widely attributed; reflects ideas in the *Corpus Hippocraticum* (compiled 5th-4th century BCE).

UniSA (University of South Australia): Smiling and brain activity study, *Experimental Psychology* (2020).

PART SEVEN

Rosenthal, R., & Jacobson, L. (1968): *Pygmalion in the Classroom.* Holt, Rinehart & Winston.

Viktor Frankl: *Man's Search for Meaning* (1946 Beacon Press)

Bruce Lee: *Striking Thoughts: Bruce Lee's Wisdom for Daily Living* (Tuttle Publishing, 2002)